Lewis Clements

Shooting Adventures, Canine Lore and Sea-Fishing Trips

Vol. II.

Lewis Clements

Shooting Adventures, Canine Lore and Sea-Fishing Trips
Vol. II.

ISBN/EAN: 9783337145378

Printed in Europe, USA, Canada, Australia, Japan

Cover: Foto ©Andreas Hilbeck / pixelio.de

More available books at **www.hansebooks.com**

SHOOTING ADVENTURES

CANINE LORE

AND

SEA-FISHING TRIPS

BY

"WILDFOWLER," "SNAPSHOT."

(*Of "The Field."*)

In Two Volumes.

VOL. II.

LONDON:
CHAPMAN AND HALL, 193, PICCADILLY, W.
1879.

TABLE OF CONTENTS.

CANINE LORE.
(*Continued.*)

	PAGE
SHOOTING WITH BEAGLES	3
A PREVENTIVE OF HYDROPHOBIA	10
DROWNING DOGS	14
ANECDOTES OF SPORTING DOGS	21
COURSING IN FRANCE	27
BUYING AND SELLING DOGS	33
CURIOSITIES OF FRENCH CANIOLOGY. I.	40
,, ,, ,, II.	47
FRENCH HOUNDS	53

Table of Contents.

	PAGE
ALGERIAN GREYHOUNDS	61
PARADING PRIZE DOGS	69
WOLF-SHOOTING IN FRANCE	73
FRENCH OFFICIAL WOLF-HOUNDS. I.	74
,, ,, ,, II.	82
CONTINENTAL POINTERS AND SETTERS	88
CONTINENTAL BOAR-HOUNDS. I.	97
,, ,, II.	104
BOAR AND WOLF HUNTING	111
THE WORKING OF SPORTING DOGS AT FIELD TRIALS AND IN THE FIELD. I.	119
,, ,, ,, ,, ,, ,, II.	127
,, ,, ,, ,, ,, ,, III.	136
,, ,, ,, ,, ,, ,, IV.	146
A DAY'S WILDFOWLING ON THE ORWELL	161
A SECOND DAY'S WILDFOWLING ON THE ORWELL	168

Table of Contents.

SEA-FISHING TRIPS.

	PAGE
FILEY BRIG	175
SCARBOROUGH AND WHITBY	186
OFF THE NORTH FORELAND AND OFF THE BLACK ROCK	197
OFF THE SOUND	208
IN THE DOWNS AND OFF THE SOUTH FORELAND	218
FROM PORTSMOUTH TO THE NEEDLES	227
SPITHEAD AND HAYLING ISLAND	238
BARN ROCKS, BOGNOR ROCKS, AND THE PARK	251
BOULOGNE-SUR-MER	259

CANINE LORE
(Continued).

CANINE LORE
(*Continued*).

SHOOTING WITH BEAGLES.

THE fact that beagles are such great favourites with practical gunners, lies in their great stoutness and truthfulness. A well-bred beagle who opens can be depended upon as telling no lies; he has found, and this he stoutly and emphatically proclaims, and forthwith sets himself to the task of bringing the quarry out of its stronghold, to encounter the guns. If the shooters allow the quarry to escape, the little hound demurely follows its track with the unremitting energy of a bloodhound.

Beagles are the cheapest dogs in use, with or without the gun. The price of a beagle rarely exceeds five pounds, and to reach that figure the animal must indeed be a very good one. Of course, there are beagles and beagles; but, any fancy price given for a dog does not prove, *per se*, that it is a better animal than its neighbour may be, though at a far lower figure. A good beagle may be had for a couple of pounds at any time, and this, I argue, is not dear, considering the intrinsic qualities of the animal.

I should not, certainly, advocate the use of these dogs indiscriminately, in and out of place; but, when a man lives in a thorny, bushy, wild sort of a country, full of fur, in small coverts, where pointers and setters would be practically useless, then he cannot do better than provide himself with beagles.

Beagles of experience are intelligent. I have had several with which I could go pheasant-shooting, as well as rabbit or hare shooting. This, of course, is a matter of private understanding brought about by a long intercourse between master and dogs.

The number of beagles required for carrying on successfully a shooting programme, depends entirely on the nature of the ground to be tried. If you have only hedgerows, or pastures overgrown with bushes, a couple of beagles are just as many as one man can conveniently follow. More would only bother the shooter; for these hounds have a will of their own, and if they should chance to hit separately on different scents, the odds are a thousand to one that they will, each of them, follow its own find, and (you know the proverb: do not hunt two hares at once) you will, most likely, hesitate between the two or three different lines of action, and succeed in tiring yourself pretty considerably and bagging nothing. Two beagles, accustomed to one another, on the other hand, generally stick and "find" together; or, if one finds and says so, the other unhesitatingly gives up his own search, and flies to his comrade's side, ascertains the truth of his call, and, there you are, all working with perfect *ensemble* and good understanding.

But, if your coverts are somewhat large and strong, two dogs cannot possibly do justice to them. In this case, four beagles or more—in fact, any reasonable number above two couple, will be about "the thing."

Great care should be taken that no wires have been set in such coverts as are to be drawn by beagles; for, however comparatively harmless a "wire" may be to a large dog, it is quite another pair of shoes when a small hound gets caught; for whereas a large dog will be caught by the leg, the little dog will be "wired" by the neck, and, as beagles are proverbially stubborn animals, the wretched beast, in its frantic endeavours to escape or break the noose, will strangle itself. This, though frequent, does not always happen. Those beagles of mine, of whom I made mention just now, were so accustomed to being caught that they remained still, whining all the while till released. Even large dogs do not always escape with slight injuries. I once saw a setter bitch caught by her fore-leg. She was at some distance from us, and, instead of acting as my beagles would have done, she not unnaturally struggled fiercely to get loose, and actually bared her leg of its skin for more than two inches before we could reach her and set her free. Had this bitch been caught round the neck, she would have seriously injured herself, if not strangled herself outright; therefore too much caution cannot be used in preserving carefully coverts that are usually tried by small dogs, whether spaniels or beagles.

Now about the colour of beagles. A great deal has been said in favour of the hare-pied dogs. I tried some of these, together with hound-marked ones, black ones, black and white ones, white ones, &c. &c., and upon my conscience I never found the hare-pied beagles one *iota* better, in any respect, than the others. But, on the other hand, I found that their colour materially interfered with the shooter's peace of mind, particularly when the dogs were employed for rabbit-shooting; their *dead-leaves* colour made them so very *inconspicuous*, if I may use this expression, that it was positively impossible to decide when anything rushed by, in the furze—whether it was a dog, or a hare or rabbit. And as a matter of fact, in the course of my shooting experience, I witnessed something like a score of these dogs being accidentally shot in such circumstances; and in that number there certainly were at least fifteen or sixteen whose colour, closely resembling that of their quarry, had been the immediate cause of their death.

From all this I draw the conclusion that, although the colour of a sporting dog matters but little beyond the fancy of its owner if the dog is a large one, it is of the utmost importance that all small dogs employed with the gun should be of as startling a colour as can be found, and that all uniformly brownish or yellowish coloured dogs, if small, should be discarded, for the safety of the animals themselves.

If white beagles could be had, I think this colour would be the most desirable as far as *safety* be concerned. At any rate any beagles or small spaniels with plenty of white about their bodies are about safe from being shot; but a small patch of white is almost their death-warrant. The sportsman catches a glimpse of this little patch, imagines that it is the white of the tail of a hare or a rabbit breaking away, and straightway floors the dog.

The training of beagles is very simple; but, before I proceed to describe it, I would just like to give a friendly hint to my brother-sportsmen, and that is, not to enter their young hounds until they are strong and full-grown, and otherwise capable of enduring the great hardships of their calling. These little "miniatures" have an exhausting work before them, and, being constitutionally very nervous and excitable, I find that, if entered too young, the excitement they undergo is apt to bring on fits. Therefore I should not advise a beagle to be entered, at any rate, before nine or ten months old. If a couple of months older, so much the better.

Now the best way I have found to train them is to procure a few wild rabbits, and as it is most important that the dog should eventually reach the game, young rabbits are preferable to the full-grown ones. Put them in a bag, and, taking one of your beagles with you (mind, one only at a time), repair to a field where the grass and weeds have been allowed to grow wild—the thicker the better, as it is important that the dog should hunt by "nose" alone. When on the ground, put round the dog's neck a collar, to which a string of three or four yards in length is fastened, and then take out one of the rabbits, show it to the dog, allow him to smell it, and the moment he opens his mouth to make a grab at it (which he is sure to do sooner or later) put the rabbit down on the ground before the dog, and let it go. Of course the beagle will immediately evince a violent wish to follow it. But you must not let him go freely as yet. Let him hunt the trail, but keep him on his cord, and make him follow the scent step by step, checking his eagerness whenever he overruns the track in his anxiety to reach the animal ; but, when he *fairly* reaches it, through *sheer hunting*, and *not by mere accident*, if you can spare the rabbit, let the dog kill it. It will for the future give him a zest for his work.

Some men even go so far as to let the dog eat the rabbit. They contend, rightly, that it makes him the more eager for a hunt afterwards. I know it does; but often the dogs thereby contract the vile habit of eating their game. Now this, sooner or later, must prove very annoying; for, a man who does not mind sacrificing, now and then, a head of game for his beagles, does not like to have every hare or rabbit he shoots forthwith torn to pieces or even eaten, *as a matter of course*, by his dogs. Therefore I should recommend trainers and sportsmen to forego such a system of training. A good hound lets his dead quarry alone, barring, perhaps, a good licking of its fur, for self-gratification at having brought it to its end.

The second lesson consists in letting go another rabbit, *unperceived* by the dog, and then putting him on the scent, and urging him to follow it. If he does so successfully, your young hound knows all you can teach him for the present, and there remains nothing now for you to do but to take him out a-hunting in earnest.

These lessons must be given to every dog separately. Some trainers who enter a lot of hounds together generally succeed in having one or two leaders in the pack, and all the rest become mere followers, who are at a *nonplus* when the leaders are absent or sick. Such should not be the case. Every individual hound ought to hunt on his own hook, and ought not to trust blindly to his companions. When *each one* does his work, truly then have you a fine pack.

In conclusion, I would hint to "beaglemen" that, not only must their dogs be trained to hunt, but that they must not be gun-shy. Therefore they should not wait till the dogs are old to make them acquainted with the noise of firearms; if they do delay too much, they may find themselves in the same fix as I was once. I had had four young beagles given me, at the beginning of my shooting career. But alas! after having carefully trained them, I took them to a small wood, from which they bolted a hare, which I shot. So far so good. But lo! to my astonishment, no beagles made their appearance. I looked round, and behold! they were running away, with their tails between their legs: *Honteux comme un renard qu'une poule aurait pris.* Poor little fellows, it was not their fault, it was mine; I had entirely overlooked that part of their education, and I had some trouble to reconcile them to it. I need not say that such a thing never afterwards happened to me again.

To accustom young dogs to the gun, I should let pistol-shots be fired, frequently, in their yard. They soon get reconciled to it, especially if caressed or fed at the same time, and afterwards they see that the gun is their ally.

There is no kind of shooting more exhilarating than shooting with beagles, and I think it is but fair to say a word in favour of our little beauties. I am sure, if this should chance to meet the eyes of a beagleman, he will heartily endorse my opinion.

A PREVENTIVE OF HYDROPHOBIA.

SOME years ago I was on a visit to a friend who lived near the Forest of Haguenau, in Alsace. He, too, was an enthusiastic shooter, and every moment he could spare he devoted to sport. We were at it sometimes for days from sunrise till sunset. Well, one day he had gone on business to the town, and on his return he informed us that some strange dogs suffering from hydrophobia were about, that he had heard it announced at the sound of drums in the streets of the town; and that bills had been posted everywhere in the villages, warning the good peasants to be on the look-out. This was bad news for us, for we did not like running the risk of getting any of our dogs bitten, and for two or three days we went shooting by ourselves, leaving the dogs at home. The sport, however (as well may be imagined), was wonderfully tame, and though Fritz, my friend's keeper, did his best with his stick and his shouts, we made but poor bags, and accordingly we grew very despondent. Meanwhile we had seen no strange dogs about, and finally we resolved to have a cast on the following day. There was, half a mile from the house and a mile from the village, a small covert that had not as yet been disturbed, and we agreed to hunt the said covert with both our packs together. I had at the time four dachshunds, my friend had seven, and the next morning early we sallied forth, followed by our long-legged Fritz holding them in leash. We met the *garde-forestier* on our way. He had heard about a mad dog, he said, and was going about with his gun in the hope of settling him, but he had not seen it as yet.

Well, to cut matters short, we reached the wood and took our stations, whilst Fritz was taking the hounds round. I was standing at a corner facing two sides of the wood, and a path cut across it, so that if anything stirred I had a pretty chance of bagging. Well, I heard the dachs hitting on a track, so I cocked my gun and stood on the *qui vive*, with my eyes pretty well skinned I can assure you. By-and-by the hounds crossed the path in full cry, but they were going away from me, and two moments after I heard, bang! from my friend's gun; the hounds' voices redoubled in energy, then they stopped, and I heard Fritz swearing at them; evidently he was getting the quarry out of their way. Then the pack was brought in again, and the same play re-enacted; but that time I was favoured. The cry came closer and closer to me, under the thick covert, and out jumped a roebuck about forty yards from me. I fired at him and he dropped. Before he had time to recover, the leading dachshund was hanging from his neck, and the others hastened to the rescue. Whilst they did so, however, I noticed that they, one and all, looked in the dry ditch that surrounded the wood, and, apparently frightened, turned somewhat out of their course, with their tails between their legs, and with fear and terror depicted in their movements, until they had passed the place, when, resuming their course, they would "open" again, until each had reached the buck. Now, anyone who has had the handling of dachshunds in packs knows that it takes something to frighten them, for, forsooth, they will fight with you, their own master, if you snatch their game from them; so I was wondering what it could be that evidently scared them so, and I was going towards the place to ascertain its nature, when the last *hund* coming up with a dash in his hurry to be with the others, tumbled in the ditch, and there he was set upon instantly, for he howled and scrambled out as fast as he could. I got near then, and saw a strange dog snarling about among the briars. I opened the breech of my gun, shoved in two large-shot cartridges, walked up to him, and blew his head off.

Fritz and my friend then came up, wondering what the three shots meant; and the now dead dog proved to be a shepherd's dog, that had been bitten some time before and had disappeared. We instantly collared the dachs that had just been bitten by him; we muzzled him with a strap; I opened with a penknife one of my cartridges, emptied the powder over the wounds in his shoulder and leg, and striking a match I set fire to the powder. The dog kicked considerably, but nevertheless we repeated the performance three times. He walked lame for a day or two, but soon got over it, and to this day he never has had an attack, and to the best of my belief he never will have. There is nothing like gunpowder for a suspicious bite. It goes into the wound well, and scarifies it thoroughly. I daresay a red-hot iron is very good too; but the point at issue I believe in all such cases is *prompt*, and, if possible, *instantaneous action*. Now when you are miles away, perhaps, from a house, it is not easy to procure a red-hot iron, whereas a sportsman has always gunpowder, and generally some matches, and that is all that is needed.

I should, however, always advocate the muzzling of the patient, because, though perhaps involuntarily, in the passing pain he will try to bite you. At least I have always seen them try to do so, and I have treated myself over a score of dogs thus in suspicious cases. I have never had a mad dog, and I have owned a considerable number. Let sportsmen adopt this system ; it is the quickest and most certain in its effect. Let them fire the wound rather three times than one ; it is safer, though momentarily unpleasant, both to the sportsman who has to do it to his favourite, and to the dog who endures the pain. But it is all for his good, and all for the best.

DROWNING DOGS.

SEVERAL sporting articles which I have read lately have brought back to my mind some striking incidents of shooting life; among these, that of the death of one dog by, and the narrow escape of another from, drowning.

The first mishap happened as follows : We had been out punting one night, and had been particularly successful in our sport, so that, as a matter of course, punt retriever was very tired and regularly knocked up. We were coming home in the morning, when, a bunch happening to cross our bows, I knocked over a widgeon; the dog flew overboard, and landing on a sunken rock, got crippled. Now the wind had risen considerably, so that when the bird fell it was carried away with some speed both by the tide and the wind, and it was all that the dog could do to reach it. But now came the tug of war, for the lamed animal had to contend against the heavy waves, the tide was against him, and the wind straight in his teeth. He struggled on gamely for a minute or so, whilst we pulled towards him with all our might, when it became apparent that the dog was being fast drifted among the shallows, where we dared not follow him with our boat, on account of the sunken rocks. We then turned towards land, and called out lustily to the dog to try and follow our direction. He heard us, for he turned his head towards us, and I shall never forget the despair depicted on the unfortunate dog's countenance. He was then paddling heavily, evidently being knocked out of time, and his pursed-up lips, wild eyes, and dripping face, plainly told that he had virtually given up the contest, and that his motions were all but mechanical.

I do not mind acknowledging the fact that, had a man been getting drowned under my eyes, I could not possibly have been more powerfully moved; and when, after two or three duckings, the head of the dog did not reappear, and we knew that his fate was sealed, we looked at each other mournfully, and, under the pretence of a sudden cold, we all, inexplicably and unaccountably, began to cough and blow our noses. But it was all bosh!—the three of us were snivelling, only we did not like to show it; but, all the same, I know that my heart was so big that I could not breathe, and I felt so desponding that I inwardly cursed my stars for having fired at the wretched widgeon—cause of all the mischief.

The next day the dog's body was found at low tide among the rocks, and we buried him decently, as a good, trusty, and faithful servant ought to be.

"Poor devil!" said our puntsman, as he began throwing some earth over the box that contained the now lifeless body, "that was a cruel death; but," he added, throwing proudly another spadeful, "all the same, he nabbed the bird, did he not? He could not have made a better end."

This sally brightened us a bit, and other events soon partly blotted out the memory of our old Nigger. Many years then passed on; shooting seasons succeeded each other rapidly, each bringing along with it its fair share of incidents, accidents, pleasures, and tribulations ; when, some years ago, as I was shooting over a marsh during the hard frost of a hard winter, another dog of mine nearly got drowned.

This is how it happened. The marsh lies between some narrow downs bordering the sea and the fields. Usually, this marsh is comparatively dry—that is to say, the cattle-feeding ground is kept carefully drained, and all the water is securely confined into natural and artificial ditches and canals ; but that year there had fallen such a quantity of rain that everything had been completely flooded, and, the frost just then supervening, the marsh became one sheet of ice. Not a very nice state of things, this, for a shooter! However, what one cannot help one must put up with, and I had to act up to that motto, whether I liked it or not.

One day, then, after having shot for a couple of hours over the fields, and having found but little therein to satisfy my killing propensities, I bethought myself of going into the downs, and there knocking over a few rabbits.

I had a friend shooting with me that day, and he, being a heavy fellow, did not care about venturing his weight on the ice ; so it was agreed that we should go round, he taking the east side of the marsh, and I the west, so as to be able to pick up any stray birds that might have sought shelter behind the willow-trees, low banks, and hedges.

We accordingly separated. My friend had with him a black-and-white setter bitch named Countess, and I had a brown pointer dog answering to the harmonious name of Click. He had been so called on account of his extraordinary sharpness, even in his puppyhood, in distinguishing among any other noises the cocking or uncocking of a gun's hammers. It was a standing practical joke in our household, when the dog was fast asleep before the large kitchen chimney, to noiselessly take up a gun and to click the locks, when, as if galvanised, the dog would jump up to his feet and rush with alacrity to the man who held the weapon.

With such a predilection for firearms, the dog was bound to become a proficient adept in the art of fowling, and I daresay I had shot over him, at the time of the accident of which I am now speaking, a round four or five thousand heads of game. The dog was eight years old, and had been my constant companion wherever I went, with or without the gun; so that he and I made *la paire*, and where the dog was seen, everybody, for ten miles round the house, knew that *I* was not far off. In truth, I *loved* that dog—there!

Well, *pour revenir à notre aventure*, on my way to the downs I sprang a duck, which flew off at such terrific speed that, instead of killing him outright as I ought, I only badly wounded him, and, still flying, he went and fell head first in the middle of the marsh, where I then perceived that the ice was broken, and about five square yards of water were blown into ripples by the breeze.

Now Click was a first-rate animal at retrieving from land or water (as advertisement says). Countess also was trained to do so. I, therefore, seeing the two dogs bolting towards the right place, concluded that my duck was as safe as if it were in my bag; so I stopped to watch the performance of the dogs.

Countess, who was also old in the business, wisely stopped when she heard the ice cracking under her feet, and her master whistled her back at once. But Click went splash in the water like a brick, and almost jumped on the duck's back. The bird, however, was not dead as yet, and by a final struggle it dived and disappeared under the ice. The dog, who knew the trick, kept wisely where he was, ready to nab the bird on its reappearance at the surface of the water; but no bird reappeared. Evidently its strength had gone; it had not been able to swim back, and had died under the ice. I then called back the dog, and he, perhaps also aware that any further waiting would be useless, and at any rate no doubt tired with swimming in the bargain, answered readily to the call and swam to the ice; but there, to my consternation and horror, he in vain tried to hook his claws into it. He tried again and again, but repeatedly failed and fell back in the water. I saw that he was becoming fast exhausted; already his lips were strangely pursed up, like those of poor Nigger of old; and he looked at me, oh—so strangely! Blind love, a mute appeal, an absolute despair were all mingled together in that one last fond look at his master.

By that time my friend had run up to me, and Countess (who says that animals have no souls?)—Countess had run to the brink of the hole where her old companion was slowly dying, and she howled and howled so terribly and so strangely that it froze the very marrow in my bones.

"Look here," said I hurriedly to my friend, "take my gun."

"What for?"

"I cannot stand this, and I will rescue the dog."

"You will do nothing of the kind," said he. "Stay here; the ice cannot bear your weight. Come back!" He shouted as I commenced my perilous journey, and he began tearing his hair wildly.

By that time two shepherds who were in the downs had

run down to the marsh's edge, and they too besought me to go back.

But, bless you, I did not care, and did not even listen. The sight of my poor Click drowning there, inch by inch, before my eyes, and the remembrance of Nigger, nerved me to do anything.

The ice began cracking; then I lay on my hands and knees, and went crawling thus as fast as I could.

The old dog saw me.

"Cheer up, Click! cheer up! I am coming!" I shouted wildly.

Countess ran then to me, I remember well; she licked my face, impeded my way, and I am afraid she made me swear. But, poor bitch, she did all this with a good intention, and I had not the heart to punish her. However, I pushed her aside, and went on, when crick! crack! the ominous sound told me that the ice was breaking. I felt my knees and my hands getting wet; then the piece of ice on which I was broke, and down I went; but, thank Heaven! not deep. The marshes were flat, and I then bethought myself that there could not be more than four feet of water; so I resolutely pushed forward, breaking the ice on my way, till I reached my old dog, half dead and considerably damp—notwithstanding which latter uncomfortable state, I took him and hugged him in my arms and brought him back safely to shore. Then we all ran home, and very thankful I was when I found myself wrapped up in blankets, and steaming before half-a-dozen logs blazing away merrily in the large country chimney.

When this adventure became known among our neighbours, some of them blamed me, others said I had done right. At any rate, one thing is certain, and it is this—

that, should such an unlucky event happen again, I should do just the same over again; for, nothing, to my mind, is more heartrending than witnessing such a slow death as drowning, especially when the accident happens to the dog out of obedience to your orders, in the furtherance of a pleasurable pursuit.

A dog that gets shot is put out of trouble at once, but a dog who is getting drowned is a sight never to be forgotten when it has been once witnessed.

ANECDOTES OF SPORTING DOGS.

SOME six or seven years ago, during a summer trip to Ostend, I witnessed with some astonishment the following incident :—Close to the beginning of the wooden jetty, near the sea-wall, was a small wooden house, occupied at the time by a beerhouse keeper, and I had had my attention more than once drawn to the place on account of the large number of sporting dogs that were continually about the house. There were pointers, setters, and greyhounds, over a dozen, besides some puppies. Subsequently I was told that the man dealt in sporting dogs, which explained this unusual congregation, and henceforth, barring an occasional glance at the dogs when I happened to be passing by, I paid but little attention to the man, or to his proceedings. But one morning, as I was going towards the end of the jetty for a little sea-fishing, I caught sight of Lord B. (with whom I was acquainted) walking with the beerhouse keeper on the sands, and both going towards the Kursaal. Two greyhounds were trotting behind the man, and he appeared to me to be carrying something in his arms which, from the distance at which I stood, I could not make out, but, as several people at once congregated, and followed the party, evidently with the prospect of some treat in store, I abandoned for the time being my walk to the pier, and went to see what was going to take place. Judge, then, of my astonishment, friendly reader, when, on getting near, and joining Lord B. for an explanation, he told me that they were going to have a coursing match!

"These two greyhounds," he explained to me, pointing to the dogs, "are extraordinary good ones in the field. They rarely, if ever, miss their quarry; to that I can personally testify, for I have seen them at work pretty often, when the man has acted as guide to me in my shooting and coursing excursions. Now, the most extraordinary thing is, that when thus engaged in *bona-fide* sporting runs, they are desperate dogs, and invariably kill their hare as soon as they lay hold of it; but now they are going to catch one, and bring it back alive. Come and see. It will be good fun."

Well, of course I went with them, and when we arrived before the Kursaal the man put down a tame hare, and she sat up, and looked about quite unconcernedly, the two greyhounds, meanwhile, watching her very earnestly. Their master then clapped his hands noisily, for a signal, and away went the hare at full speed, with the two greyhounds in pursuit. They never attempted to catch her at first, but bundled her about with their muzzles, ran ahead of her, and bothered her so that they finally stopped her, when one of them picked her up in the gentlest possible manner, and, bringing her back to his master, placed her at his feet. After shaking herself, the hare again sat up, as though nothing extraordinary had happened! The two dogs meanwhile seemed to enjoy the fun immensely. They jumped about and barked at the hare, poking her with their noses, to make her run again, I suppose; and altogether it was the most extraordinary sight for a sportsman to witness. There were by that time hundreds of people around us, and, at their entreaty, the man gave another exhibition of the funny coursing. This over, he explained to us that the hare was quite tame, it was always loose about his place, and none of his dogs ever attempted to molest her. So far so good. If the dogs who ever attempted to bite her, or to kill her, were at once well beaten, of course they would henceforth desist from trying anything of the sort again ; but to make the two working and usually desperate greyhounds catch her and retrieve her without hurting her, was a most extraordinary and most entertaining piece of business.

I am sorry to say that some little time after, a stranger going by with a gun, saw the hare in the downs near the man's house, and shot her, thinking she was *feræ naturæ*. The said sporting stranger narrowly escaped a tremendous licking, but an explanation and a compensation being handsomely given, there the matter ended.

Now this instance of forbearance on the part of working greyhounds is truly astonishing, when one takes into consideration that, as a rule, such dogs show no mercy to whatever they course. I have had many dogs myself, and I must confess that sometimes I could hardly refrain from marvelling at the intelligence actually displayed by some of them. One of my retrieving pointers was, under ordinary circumstances, of the most amiable disposition, being ready to fawn on anybody, and allowing anyone to pat him, to pull his ears, &c. &c.; but in the pursuit of sport no such nonsense would he allow, and the extreme pride and jealousy he invariably exhibited when he had picked up some game I had shot, and was bringing it to me, were almost laughable to behold. Woe betide, then, anyone who dared to interfere with him, in any way whatsoever! This characteristic of his I was well aware of, but I had no idea as to what extent he might push it to, when one day, in Norfolk, he gave me a grand illustration thereof. He had pointed a hare in her form, I had kicked puss out of it, and shot at her, but had only succeeded in wounding her, and away she went. Well, the keeper and I kept our eyes on her, and we distinctly saw that, when going up the hill, she faltered, then stopped, then crawled on, and barely had strength left her to disappear behind the fence. I then sent on the dog to fetch, and off he went. He roaded the hare to the very identical spot in the hedge through which she had gone, and we therefore made up our minds to have it soon in the game-bag; but a minute went by, then two, then three, and no dog coming back, we went to see what had happened, and lo and behold! standing on the bank of the road, in the hollow, was a gipsy, brandishing a cudgel and kicking away like steam at the dog. But the latter would not be denied, and kept in front of him, showing his teeth and bristling all over. When we appeared on the scene the man saw it was all "up," and flinging down the hare, which he had hidden under his coat, he bolted down the lane, looking back once or twice as though in fear of the dog, I presume. But the pointer did not pay him the slightest attention. He picked up the hare, and brought it to us without any more ado.

The most entertaining dog I have ever possessed, however, was a small setter I bought in France. She was most marvellously well-trained for sport, and could perform all sorts of amusing tricks besides. For instance, if anyone's hat or handkerchief happened to be blown away by the wind, no matter where, on land or on water, she would instantly go to fetch it when told. At home she would go and look for my slippers the moment she saw I was unlacing my boots. She would bring my boots, leggings, game-bag, parcels of cartridges, anything in fact that was pointed out to her; and if I lost anything, purposely or not, when in the field, I had but to tell her that I had lost something, to go and fetch it, when she would retrace my footsteps until she came to what I had dropped.

I remember once when, with a large-bore muzzle-loading gun, I was wildfowl-shooting on the coast, I left my powder-flask on some rock and missed it soon afterwards. I looked everywhere for it myself at first, but could not find it anywhere about. Then the thought struck me to send Finette for it. And away she went, walking wherever I had walked until she came to a place where I had a short time before hid in ambush, and she came back with the flask.

Of course a sportsman never parts with such a dog. I had once a fair sum offered me for her, and had almost agreed to take it, but at the last moment I begged to be released from my half-promise, and she lived and died in my service.

One of her daughters was also extremely clever. Even when quite a puppy she showed a wonderful aptitude and a remarkable intelligence. At the very beginning of her sporting career she was caught once by the paw in a wire set by a poacher for hares. Of course when she pulled desperately to get loose, she naturally tightened the noose all the more, and her howling was terrible. I ran to the rescue, loosened the wire, and pocketed the snare. The setter, however, was lamed for a day or two. About a fortnight after the little one ran her paw again clean through another loop when going through a hedge. Do you imagine that she pulled then to release herself? Not she. She set up a very noisy whine, and waited until I came to her. Now I call that a very sensible proceeding on her part. Had she straightened the noose, she might have lamed herself for life that time.

The instinct for sport in good sporting dogs is strong, even unto death. I have had an old dog, totally blind of one eye, and very filmy in the other, as deaf as a post, and as stiff as a poker (through innumerable rheumatisms all over his limbs and body), who would try to dance about me when he saw a gun in my hands! His attempts at youthful sprightliness were ludicrous in the extreme, but they almost made tears come to my eyes more than once. I ought to have had him shot or poisoned for his own sake, poor fellow; but he had been a good and faithful servant to me, and I had not the heart to have him done away with. Nay, once he came on the sea-shore with me and went to sea after a bird, but when he got it he could not see land, and did not know which way to come back. He kept on turning about with his poor blind eye opened to the utmost as if it could see better then, and, foreseeing that the old boy would inevitably get drowned, I waded in after him. He did not hear me, or see me coming, and when I touched him he turned suddenly his only available " peeper " on me, and it said as plainly as ever eye could speak: " Master, I had given up seeing you again, and I am *so* glad!"

He gave up his doggy ghost some time after. We found him dead one morning on a sock of mine. The very day before he wanted to go shooting, albeit he could hardly stand.

COURSING IN FRANCE.

IN *The Sporting Gazette* I observed once a very plausible query, viz.: Why public coursing should not, practically, be introduced into France? I fear that some considerable time will elapse before this most pleasurable pastime will have taken sufficient root in our Gallic neighbours' land to warrant the establishment of official meetings. France is, and has always been, under a proverbially red-tape government, so that changes of any kind whatsoever, in the routine either of sport or business, are mighty slow in making way against the existing *encroutées* notions, and as greyhounds are forbidden *in toto* now, why it is hard to tell when they will ever have a chance of making their *début*, even if the French sportsmen were to claim their introduction. Very little notice, as a rule, is taken of the wishes of mere subjects in all continental countries, but in France this indifference on the part of the Government towards its *administrés* is carried to the utmost extent. Therefore, although many French sportsmen who have become surreptitiously acquainted with the qualities of greyhound should heartily back up any proposed reversal of the sporting laws that forbid the use of the long-tails in the field, there is not as yet the slightest tendency shown by Government to gratify their harmless wish in that respect.

Some years ago, when I had gone to France for the sea-bathing season, I was induced to take out a game-license and go shooting. It was in the north, a few miles from Dunkerque, where the country is remarkably flat, and free from any awkward obstacles that might interfere with a view of the sport, if any were carried on. The thought struck me, the moment I set foot in these fields, what an excellent coursing-ground one might find in that part of the country, at any rate at least as far as the ground itself was concerned, for the hares are not by any means now sufficiently numerous to warrant the presence, at any one time, of more than two or three brace of first-rate performers; but this could soon be improved, and I am sure that, were the ground to be well preserved for a couple of years, there would be no fur importation required in order to make the place fit for a first-class meeting. However, even at the time I am speaking of, one could bag (with the gun, mind) four or five brace of hares in a good day's sport. Now I don't call that bad at all, when there is plenty of feather as well to vary the monotony of the sport; but had we had greyhounds, we might have coursed, I undertake to say, eight or nine brace of hares in the course of a morning.

I expressed, of course, my astonishment at the absence of longtails in the field, and it was then that I was informed that their use was forbidden. Now everyone knows how sweet forbidden fruit is; and when I mentioned to my quondam companions what our greyhounds can do and will do, when in good trim, my eulogium was met with the inquiry whether I could get one or two over, just to see their performance.

"But what about the law?" I asked, somewhat amused at the eagerness of my French friends.

This was met with the retort, politely delivered, "*Que le diable emporte la loi!*"

After such a decisive settlement of the question, there remained for me nothing to do but to get over one or two fair "dusters," and I wrote to England on the same day. I knew a fellow who kept such dogs, and pretty good ones too, at least as far as the killing went, and that was all I wanted for our purpose, for it was clear that my companions expected to bag for every fair slip, and any by-play was to be out of the programme altogether. In one word, we wanted fast, clever, and, above all, quick-killing dogs.

I got what I wanted, but, as far as appearances went, I daresay the dealer would have been sadly bothered had he wanted to sell the dogs at home. They had speed, and, when they caught, their jaws held as tight as an alligator's. But they were two thoroughly experienced dogs, and, to a connoisseur, their performances savoured strongly of the lurching at times; but what were the odds so long as my friends were satisfied?

I shall never forget the interest with which the longtails were interviewed on their arrival in France. They landed at Dunkerque, where we had gone in a body to meet them. I had strongly recommended my friends the utmost secrecy, which they had sworn, with due emphasis, to keep to their dying breath. However, they had kept their word so faithfully and so well that, when the steamer drew alongside, nearly all the sporting men of the town were on the jetty to see the two much-talked-of *lévriers Anglais* disembark. This was most annoying; but *quand le vin est tiré*, *il faut le boire*, it was too late then to alter the state of things, so we went on board. I duly claimed the dogs, and they were forthwith sent home.

On the next day we made a start, and not only was the party absolutely *au grand complet*, but every available friend of ours had joined us for the fun of the thing, so that, taken all in all, we must have looked uncommonly like an invading army. The dogs had been sent over-night to the keeper's, where we found them hearty and fresh.

We were not slow in finding. A fine hare bolted out of a furze-bush, and took to the open. The two dogs made away after her, and within a few seconds fur was flying "all over the shop." A squeak, a few convulsive kicks, and No. 1 was bagged.

We were all congregated round to examine the hare and the dogs, when we were startled by a voice saying extremely distinctly, and withal very unpleasantly, "*Messieurs, je vous déclare procès-verbal !*"

We all turned round, and behold ! there was the *garde-champêtre* in all the glory of a rusty sabre, a silver medal, and a pair of canvas gaiters, coolly taking out of his pocket a greasy piece of paper and a pencil, with the evident intention of putting our names down. Vainly we remonstrated with the man, vainly we argued the matter with him over and over again. He lent a deaf ear to all our entreaties, and to whatever we could say as to his taking no notice of us, he obdurately would reply that, although he had no personal wish to be unpleasant towards us, his duty compelled him, however reluctant he might be personally, to take proceedings in the matter. Finding him so resolute in the war of words, I tried what the "golden argument" might do in the way of altering his sentiments towards us ;

so, taking a napoleon between finger and thumb, I pressed my way to the man, and, when I confronted him, the following conversation took place between us:

"My friend," I said, "of course you know very well that your prosecution would not hurt us much; the worst that could be done to us would be our being fined fifteen or twenty francs for the offence. And now, what profit should you derive from it? None whatsoever."

"But," he said, "my duty——"

"Bother your duty," I retorted warmly; "don't be a fool. Here, take this napoleon, put 'it in your pocket, and consider it as being yours, provided you agree to remain indoors, at least all the morning, until we have done here with the dogs."

"Well, sir," said the old fellow, pocketing the coin, his bit of paper, and his pencil with great alacrity, "I am very much obliged to you, but, with all due deference to your wishes, I cannot quite act to the letter of your advice."

"How? Why?"

"I am bound by my office to be out all day, so I cannot possibly go home as you wish me; but I will be off and away, and I will take care not to see you any more."

This Jesuitic way of disposing of himself set us all laughing.

The old boy went his way, and bothered us no more.

Subsequently, however, the police got wind of our little game, and we were persistently followed by gendarmes for a conviction. I heard of this in time, so I sent the dogs to a friend, farther up the country, and he enjoyed them for some time, until, in his turn, he was fain to part with them, when he sent them to someone else, who, very likely, had also to dispose of them pretty sharp. I am convinced those two dogs gave more trouble to the authorities than all the thieves of the department put together. Now from all this I infer that there must be something wrong in that state of things in France. The country, not only round about Dunkerque, but in many parts of France, is eminently fit for coursing, and the French, were they allowed freely to enjoy the sport, would take to it, not only kindly, but greedily. Of course, official coursing meetings might be speedily arranged, but the first point to be attended to would be the repeal of the prohibitory law which peremptorily forbids the use of the dogs in the land. This unreasonable law, by-the-way (like all things arbitrary), is already evaded on a pretty large scale, inasmuch as a fair percentage of the so-called French *chiens de chasse* are nothing more nor less than lurchers, bred with long ears (so as to be physically out of the prohibitory clause), but practically answering the purpose of greyhounds, to the best of their abilities.

BUYING AND SELLING DOGS.

As I have had some experience in buying and selling dogs, perhaps an outline of the transactions will prove interesting as well as instructive.

The trouble arises chiefly with sporting dogs. A non-sporting dog offers no great difficulty. There he is, and if you like him you buy him, and all is over. But a sporting dog must have a good nose (and this you can't find out by looking at him); he must have bottom (and that requires trying); he must have sense (one in a dozen has some, and the rest none); and he must be well broken. If this be so, then indeed you have a dog fit to be called a sporting dog.

But how many are there such? I have, in my time, sold and bought, and indeed, now buy and sell, many pointers, setters, spaniels, and retrievers, but, "would you be surprised to hear" that I have had to try a thousand before I could muster a hundred? Yet this is the plain fact. Therefore a word to the innocent. When a man tells you that his dog is perfect, and, being unknown to you, asks you to send him your cheque in advance, be wise, and keep your money. Seeing is believing; manage to run the dog if you cannot trust the man. Try the animal well yourself, and be sure that your deposit is secure. When you know the seller, the case is different; no man in his senses, if he has any standing, will care to deceive anyone, even if the thought came into his head, since he can always be found, and made to recoup; therefore, if possible (and it is always possible), deal with some responsible party (and there are many such); then you are safe. Although dealing in sporting dogs is generally an undertaking of a serious nature, it must not be inferred that the comic element is eliminated therefrom. Far from it. And, to a man with a genuine fund of humour, there is generally a good deal coming uppermost in numerous transactions which will excite comments of a varied and occasionally amusing nature. I remember once a very entertaining piece of business, in which I was the sufferer, but that did not prevent me from enjoying the fun. Some six or seven years ago I received a letter one morning from a correspondent, requesting me to forward him, without delay, a black-and-tan setter bitch of mine. I had bought her originally from a man who had a weakness for "docking" his sporting dogs, hence she had only about a foot of tail. She was, however, a good one, and I sent her away with a good character. Judge of my astonishment when the next day came the following epistle:

"MY DEAR SIR,—Your man must have made a mistake. He has sent me a bob-tailed sheep-dog of the female persuasion. I have returned her, after seeing her fed and watered.—Faithfully yours, &c."

"Surely," I thought, "there must be a mistake somewhere besides the tail," and I longed to see the sort of "beast" that was being "returned." She came at last, and at first I could not recognise her at all. The handsome setter bitch had had all her "feather" clipped by some rogue on the journey, and certainly she looked more then like a drover's dog than like a setter. It took her a year to grow up her own self again, and I thereby missed her market for a whole season. At first I was, naturally enough, rather sore on the subject, but, finally, the idea of "clipping" a setter was so utterly ridiculous that I could not help laughing at the queer figure poor Bess did cut, and she did look funny, and no mistake! I can't help laughing at it even now.

Whilst on the subject of "docked" dogs, I was well "sold" once about a pointer. A gallant general wrote me for a retrieving pointer. "A French or German braque will suit me," his epistle ran, "but he must be well-bred and handsome. Why I want a foreign dog is, because foreigners break their field-dogs so well to retrieve, and that is what I require."

I accordingly wrote for the animal, and was rather dismayed when my man came in, scratching his ear thoughtfully. "I have been to fetch the dog at the station, sir," said he, "but he ain't got no tail!" And, sure enough, he had not any.

Then again, in buyers, you meet with some very remarkable people. Some folks expect a dog to work like a steam-engine, and wonder that he is not made to talk. A man slips a dog above the birds, and then is surprised that he does not point them, and that they are flushed! That man never considers the wind, and expects that, up or down wind, the dogs will scent game! Another man, whose land is as bare as a billiard-table, wonders how it is that pointers can't get a point! Another slips a brace of fast setters in a furze-field, and is surprised to find that they are speedily crippled, and want no more of it! One fires at a hare, thinks he has hit her, and sends your dogs (which he has on trial, mind) after her; then writes to say that they chase! I had a fellow once shooting a hawk, wounding it, and being much disgusted on seeing that my retrieving pointers declined picking up the ugly customer. Then you will find that no allowance is made to your dogs for change of country, of master, and of style by some people. Of course such curious persons are only in the minority. But their vagaries are, nevertheless, entertaining. Every dog sent away to be tried, or sold outright, ought to have, at first, a little drilling and humouring, to make him feel at home, especially if he is a young dog. Old dogs are not so particular. I have some now that don't care a rap who it is they go with. Show them a gun, and slip them, and they are "all there." But young dogs are not so ready to put up with strange faces and new ways, and that ought to be readily understood. The old dogs care only for sport, and don't mind who follows them. They know what they have to do, and do it; whereas the youngster remembers recent thrashings, spiked collars, and other nuisances of his education; and when he has to deal with a stranger he does not know, from his tone of voice, whether he is doing right or doing wrong, and is going to get a licking. Hence, if he is a highly-bred dog, he flings all his past tuition to the winds, and indulges to his heart's content in all sorts of vagaries, until he has cooled himself. But a sensible man ought to know that this is mere exuberance of blood and spirits, and he ought not to chastise severely such a lively youngster. If you break a dog's spirit there remains but a brute to deal with; if you treat him kindly and fairly, you make him a devoted companion.

Now that I have summarised some peculiarities of buyers, shall I enter into the strange ways of some dealers? Mind, I say some, for of course there are straightforward men in the dog-dealing trade as well as in any other business, but there is no doubt that there are a few whose ways are slightly crooked and not as they should be. To begin with, if you want to buy a dog in England to send abroad, never state that fact, because in that case some dealers will take you in; for, there exists in the minds of some of these gentry a firmly-rooted idea that anything with a dog's coat on will do for the "furriners," and they also cherish an equally firmly-rooted opinion that the said "furriner" ought to pay handsomely for the wretched specimens they condescend to supply for his especial use and delectation. Some years ago, when I was studying sporting ways in Belgium, several Belgian sportsmen asked me to get them some good dogs; I did get a few certainly, but I experienced such a deal of bother that I gave it up. Greyhounds that would not kill, pointers and setters that never would point, retrievers who swallowed their birds, wild spaniels fit only for rabbiting, and the like rubbish, were sent over to me from England with most flattering descriptions of their talents, and written warranties about a yard long, more or less, inclusive of pedigrees. The senders would not understand that, although the buyers were Belgians, they wanted really good dogs. This fact seemed to pass their comprehension, and when I returned all their rubbish, great wailing ensued. And well it might. Dogs that had been picked up for a sov. or two, which were to realise from twelve to twenty pounds each, to be returned as unsatisfactory. What an extraordinary " sell!"

Of course I did get some abuse, but not much. I am well known, and it would not do to give me, in writing or otherwise, a bullying; but I heard from exceedingly reliable sources that, verbally, I was heartily "blessed" by two or three enterprising parties. No doubt about that. What surprised me most, however, in these transactions, was that the dogs had been sent over at all, since I invariably asked them on trial for the buyers. The senders must have had a very poor opinion of the Belgians' requirements, or else thought the buyers dreadful fools, or else they must have trusted to "flukes" for the dogs to pass muster; or perhaps they themselves, the senders, did not know whether the dogs were good, bad, or indifferent. For, be it borne in mind that there are some dog-dealers, trading in sporting dogs, who know absolutely nothing about sport. Where they get their dogs from doesn't matter: sales by auction, dogs stolen, lost, or sold cheap. Anyhow, these dealers have never seen a sporting dog at work, and their notions as to what is expected of them are of the very haziest description. There was such a man in London once, who offered me a pointer for sale, and stated in his letter that we could try the dog in St. James's Park! And another Cockney wrote me that any day, if I called, I would see his spaniel setting at his tame rabbits in their hutch in Seven Dials. The invariable rule of dealers totally unknown to anybody but their own immediate admiring circle of friends is to ask for money down first, then they will send you a dog of some sort, and write out a warranty, and they are safe, generally speaking. Thousands upon thousands of pounds have thus been wasted by an over-confiding public, who really seem to long rather greedily for an opportunity to be taken in. I would repeat it: never buy but from someone you know or who is well known, if you can help it, unless you can try the dogs.

There are a few cases when a nice "deal" is to be made with town dealers; but, as a general rule, a tremendous lot of rubbish finds its way into their hands, by sales and otherwise, and a great deal of delay, trouble, and uncertainty, together with considerable expenses in rail and trials, fall to the lot of the intending buyer, who finally gets disgusted, spends pounds, and wastes weeks, to find himself after all without a dog. What I have stated here must have been the experience of all who ever had any dabbling in the buying and selling of sporting dogs, and I know there is nobody disinterested in the matter but who will thoroughly endorse what has here been stated by me.

CURIOSITIES OF FRENCH CANIQLOGY.

I.

IT was while contributing to the kennel columns of a journal that I was first led to consult the leading works on dogs published in the French tongue, and first and foremost among these came the "Histoire Physiologique et Anecdotique des Chiens de toutes les Races," by Benedict-Henry Revoil, with an introduction by no less a *littérateur* than Alexander Dumas *père*. According to his wont, Dumas rambled in his subject, and tells us, among other queer and totally new things, that St. Bernard dogs take men to the hospital just as a pointer (? retriever) brings a hare to his master! which is quite a new way of rescuing lost travellers. He then declares that Revoil's book is quite original, and, in some cases, certainly no one will contest that much; and as the book is at times rather edifying, as well as amusing, I think a few passages, taken here and there, will interest those readers who are fond of canine lore.

In his preliminary chapter Revoil makes some curious statements, having searched for them, he says, high and low, in all available records. Thus, he states that the

Egyptians of old used to weep for their dogs when they died, and buried them with grand ceremonies. He points out that Plutarch relates in his *Adversus Stoïcos* that, during his lifetime, there existed a nation who had taken a dog for their king, and all the coins of that realm were struck with the said dog's effigy. Herodotus narrates that Cyrus excused four towns from any war contributions simply because their inhabitants had spontaneously fed his dogs. Plutarch also says that Alcibiades bought one of his hounds for seven thousand drachms (about two hundred and twenty-eight pounds). Barnabo Visconti owned five hundred hounds. At Genoa there exists to this day a superb marble mausoleum erected to the memory of Andre Doria's dog. During his lifetime that dog enjoyed from Philip II., King of Spain, a pension of five hundred golden ducats, and was attended by two slaves, who served him his meals on plate. Frederick of Prussia also erected a mausoleum to his bitch Alcmène. Another bitch of his having fallen into the hands of the Austrians during a battle, he humbled himself so far as to earnestly beg of the general to send her back to him. Alexander the Great built a town in honour of a favourite deceased dog. The Emperor Adrian gave official dinners when his favourite bitch was buried; and another ordered a general fast throughout his kingdom when his dog was devoured by wolves. Charles IX. of France had a well-known favourite greyhound. Henri III. doted on poodles; Charles XII. of Sweden had his dog Pompey buried with state honours;. the Empress Catherine of Russia loved her spaniel above all things; Henry IV. of France sent his dog Fanor to Dieppe for sea-bathing, and thus made the reputation of the town as a fashionable resort—at least so says Revoil ;.

Charles X. was particularly fond of his hounds; a French duchess attired herself in deep mourning when her pet dog died; a French count did the same, and commissioned his chaplain to write an epitaph for the dog. The chaplain obeyed, and wrote:

> Ci gît Citron, qui, sans peut être,
> Avait plus de sens que son maître.
> (Here lies Citron, who, without the slightest doubt,
> Had a great deal more sense than his master.)

An Austrian countess used to rear a small army of griffons, and when one of them died she caused a mass to be sung for the repose of its soul! The Princess Ann of Wurtemberg, who lived in 1733, at Mempelgard, tortured with needles or pins one of her maids, because she had laughed at the princess's invariable custom of having all her dead dogs placed in leaden coffins. The princess, however, was prosecuted, and sentenced to transportation for five years. Newton's Diamant is too well known to readers to need any comment; Alphonse Karr had a dog named Freischütz, which used to bite him now and then; Lamartine was fond of greyhounds; Alexandre Dumas *père* had many dogs, and he described at length all their antics in his "Histoire de mes Bêtes."

Alexander II. of Russia had a favourite black setter which never left him, and Napoleon III. had his Nero, who was equally privileged to go everywhere he liked in the imperial apartments, &c. In his chapter on the "Origin of the Dog," Revoil declares that lap-dogs were unknown before the sixteenth century, and he wonders whence they came and how their deformities (*sic*) were produced. As to the origin of dogs, as a breed, he cites many opinions, all at variance, as usual, and therefore he gives no light on the subject; but he gleans, from the report of the Egyptian Commission, many interesting details. Thus, in a sarcophagus which dates from the fourth dynasty (3,400 B.C.), was found a very neat representation of a large-sized greyhound, with a collar round his neck, thereby proving that the dog (no doubt a favourite dog of the deceased) was a domesticated animal. Another tomb, which was opened at Beni-Hassan, contained sculptures depicting a sportsman with his whips and huntsmen, hunting a gazelle, and his hounds are led coupled. This tomb dates from the twelfth dynasty, or 2,300 (or thereabouts) B.C. There was no great regularity in the pack, however, for in the same couple are led a black-and-tan setter and a fawn greyhound. Some of the other hounds are, moreover, cropped, and these are, doubtless, wolfhounds or bear-hounds, whose ears have been clipped obviously for giving them some advantage over the carnivoræ when slipped against them.

Big dogs alone were held in esteem by the ancients. The Greeks could devise no handsomer gift than that of a large dog; and tradition will have it that a certain Ethiopian queen gave Alexander the Conqueror ninety enormous dogs trained for war purposes; and in an Assyrian bas-relief one may see a large dog, whose head nearly reaches the shoulder of the man who leads him. Are such monsters now quite extinct?

In the next chapter, which treats of the intelligence of dogs, Revoil gives some instances, which, taken *cum grano salis*, may do perhaps. Thus he says that a vet. having successfully set the broken leg of a dog, the said dog one day brought him a poodle chum of his, which had just broken its thigh! He also alludes, as a proof of sense in dogs, to the well-known case of a pointer and a greyhound going coursing together. The pointer's duties, of course, were to hunt for "puss," which, when once found and started, the greyhound ran down. But Revoil adds, that the pointer's master, guessing that something was wrong, placed a chain to his collar, and allowed it to drag on the ground so as to impede the dog's movements. The greyhound, however, was equal to the emergency, and he carried the dragging end of the chain in his mouth, until the pointer had found the game, when he would drop the chain and start in pursuit of the hare!

Smugglers' dogs, Revoil informs us, are of wonderful intelligence. He alludes, of course, to those which run over the French and Belgian frontiers with lace, &c. He says that when once laden with the forbidden goods, the dog assumes spontaneously his part of the responsibility. He starts when it is dark—finds out where the customs' officers are. If he meets only one on his road, he will fight him, if he cannot otherwise force his way through; but if he is not strong enough for a battle-royal, he hides himself behind a tree, or a hedge, or a wall, or a bush, and waits patiently for a favourable opportunity. Arrived at his destination, he takes care to ascertain that no one is about whom he does not know, and mistrusts, before showing himself. All this is certainly very extraordinary, if true. I need not add that thousands of these dogs are killed yearly by the customs' officers, in the execution of their duty.

Now, shepherd-dogs also exhibit a vast amount of intelligence. No one who has seen sheep-dog trials, for instance, can deny that the dog who lies down before his frightened sheep, and waits until they are quieted, then rises, and by this single movement forces them forward into the hurdles, a step at a time, does know what he is doing. He *must* know it, and he *does* know it. As soon as he has penned them all safe, his glance plainly tells, "Have I not done it well, eh?"

It is a pity such dogs can't talk.

And what about sporting dogs? There is no denying that some of them arrive at a degree of perfection and intelligence which is simply unsurpassable. In short, no matter of what breed, a well-treated dog always exhibits an amount of understanding which is, at times, quite astonishing. A well-known French sportsman and *littérateur*, Elzear Blaze, author of three or four works on shooting, relates that, one day when out shooting, he lost his way, and meeting a peasant, explained his predicament. The peasant turned round to his dog and said: "Take this gentleman to Mr. So-and-so's house, but do not yourself enter the house, come back straight here; do you hear?" Then the man explained to Mr. Blaze that he had told his dog not to enter the house, because he and the dogs there would indubitably have fought, as usual. Mr. Blaze accordingly went his way with his canine guide, who brought him to his friend's door, and then started back at full gallop on his return journey.

But the most extraordinary faculty with which dogs are endowed is that which enables them to find their way for long distances, and over roads which they have never seen before, back to certain favourite spots. Thus it is said that a dog sent from London to Scotland came back the whole way by himself, but this is rather too much, I fancy. That some hounds which have been taken leagues out of their usual beats by their quarry will find their way back to their kennels I am well aware of, as some of my own beagles, dachshunds, and harriers have repeatedly performed the feat; but between doing that much and going hundreds of miles back to their home, over an unknown country, there is a vast deal of difference, and I candidly admit that I do not believe it. Neither do I believe the concluding portion of the following tale, which Revoil narrates in his work. He says that a Parisian shoeblack had trained his dog to dip its paw into liquid mud, and when a well-dressed man came about, the dog would go to him, and putting its dirty paws on the man's well-blacked boots, would of course place him under the necessity of having the said boots blacked over again. Of course the dog's master would at once offer his services, and the trick was done. Well, an Englishman, surprised and delighted at the intelligence of the dog, bought him, and brought him to London. But (and here comes the marvellous bit) the dog, at the first opportunity, escaped, went back to the office where the conveyance which had brought him had stopped; then he followed this conveyance back to Dover, slipped on board the steamer, landed at Calais, and finally arrived in Paris, by following another conveyance! *Si non e vero, e ben trovato!*

CURIOSITIES OF FRENCH CANIOLOGY.

II.

IN his chapter on wild dogs Revoil repeats the theory that wolves are in reality but dogs, wild dogs, and not a distinct species; and, in support of this argument, he says that the proof thereof consists in the fact that one may interbreed with wolves and dogs, and the results of the crosses also procreate, thereby proving that there is no natural antipathy between the breeds. He also ranks foxes, jackals, &c., as wild dogs, and gives a summary history of the peculiarities of all known wild species, their haunts and habits. He then enters into a description of what he calls "watch"-dogs; but as he begins the list by describing shepherds' dogs, I was at first to some extent puzzled to make out the meaning of *chiens de garde*, which until then I had thought to mean only "yard"-dogs. However, he probably is right, inasmuch that certainly a shepherd's dog has to watch over sheep, &c., and therefore he is a *chien de garde* after all. According to Revoil these dogs have not altered in build; they have always been the same, according to their several breeds. This may be so in France, where local strains remain undisturbed by the introduction of any fresh blood; but here, especially since the introduction of dog shows in the canine world, many breeds have been "improved," as the word goes, until there is hardly any semblance left of the original stock. Howbeit the French seem to have a rare choice of sheep-dogs in their country.

The *chiens de Brie*, says Revoil, are fawn-coloured, and very handsome; those of *la Cran* are of a very large size, like those employed in the mountains, for obvious reasons, that of driving away any wolves or other carnivoræ who might be tempted to have a feed of mutton. The *chiens toucheurs*, I take it, are synonymous with our drovers' dogs. Revoil says that some of those *toucheurs* are so well broken that their masters trust entirely to them to take home whatever cattle or sheep they may have bought, and after giving the dogs their orders they go away upon some other business by different roads, and let the dogs take entire charge of the herds or flocks. Most of these *toucheurs* are tailless, thus corresponding with the British bob-tailed sheep-dogs. Revoil classes Pomeranians as wolf-dogs, and states that they are very large dogs; if so it is a different sort of animal to that which in our shows takes the name of Pomeranian. As watch-dogs proper Revoil enumerates the *chiens des Pyrénées* and of the Alps, redoubtable animals who fight in defence of their master or his flocks with an energy and a ferocity almost beyond belief.

We then come to St. Bernards, Newfoundlands, Labradors, *Loulous* (falsely called Pomeranians, says our author), mastiffs, *dogues de Bordeaux*, which reach an enormous size; Spanish mastiffs, used for boar-hunting, or slipped in the bull-ring when a bull's energies appear to be flagging; the *molosses*, which, crossed with bloodhounds, produced the slave-hunting dogs formerly used in America; the dogs of Thibet, the bullen-beissers or baerenbeissers employed in Germany for bear-hunting. These dogs are about the size of mastiffs, but they are far more nimble in their movements than mastiffs, and their heads greatly resemble those of bull-dogs. They will fight anything. When treating of bull-terriers and of bull-dogs, Revoil declares that "he cannot very well see their utility," but then "tastes differ." Bull-dogs were much larger years ago, he says, but although small nowadays, their courage has not diminished in any way whatsoever. It is presumable that these dogs were bred larger in times gone by with a view to the baiting of bulls and bears, which used to be public exhibitions then. Terriers and Dalmatians bring the list to an end. Dalmatians, says Revoil, show points pertaining to hound and pointer. In this I beg to differ, at least as regards modern Dalmatians, which show no hound-points at all, but are absolutely formed on the pointer model.

In the chapter devoted to the dread disease, hydrophobia, Revoil very sensibly ridicules the idea of muzzling dogs. Most muzzles, he says, do not prevent dogs from biting, but they certainly fret the dogs. He then describes the symptoms of hydrophobia, and declares that saliva alone can produce the disease. The blood of a *mad* dog (as the saying goes) inoculated to another healthy dog, produces no effect. A mad dog is dangerous before he shows any signs of rage, and the public ought to watch for the following symptoms:

"As soon as a dog feels the first effects of hydrophobia" (it is our author who speaks, and with whom remains all responsibility), "he goes into his kennel, turns surly; but at first shows no disposition to bite anyone. Soon after he becomes uneasy, restless, lies down and gets up again, as though he could not find a comfortable place to lie upon; he looks at you as though asking you to help him in his trouble, then he looks as though dazed, goes hither and thither without any perceptible end in view, lies down, gets up, fumbles about his straw with his muzzle, then he rushes to the wall as though catching flies, and finally snaps about with fury. Then he gets calmer, shuts his eyes, and seems to drop off, but soon he starts up again with a rabid howl, and darts furiously forward. A mad dog hates the sight of its usual food. Usually his tail hangs down, his mouth is open, his tongue hangs out, and is bluish in colour; the dog totters about, but he has not always saliva at the mouth. If you beat a mad dog however hard he remains silent. Moreover, healthy dogs seem to know intuitively dogs that are affected with hydrophobia, and run away from them."

Some people say, "Nothing is easier than to ascertain if a dog is mad. One has only to offer him some water. If the dog drinks, he is all right. If he refuses to do so, then there is danger." Nothing could be more fallacious. A mad dog is *not* hydrophobic—*i.e.* does not dread water; no the contrary, he tries his utmost to drink, but the contraction of his throat prevents the admission of water in his œsophagus. Nevertheless, he acts like a healthy dog— *i.e.* laps the water with his tongue, and it is difficult to see if he actually drinks it. But the main point whereby one may be warned in the case of a mad dog is by his style of barking—once heard, it is never forgotten. It is a sort of sinister howl, which goes *de crescendo*. Moreover, a mad dog at once tries to bite any other dog brought to him; and this is one of the characteristics of the disease. In the last crisis, an imprisoned mad dog bites with such recklessness at the iron bars of his cage that he frequently hurts his jaws. Paralysis invariably ends his sufferings. The only remedy as yet recommended by veterinary surgeons is an immediate and thorough cauterisation of the wound with a red-hot iron.

Lap-dogs are, according to the French author, the most inclined of the canine tribe to contract spontaneously hydrophobia, and he declares that this arises from the fact that they are refused sexual intercourse. Of course vagabond dogs are always likely to meet animals affected with the disease, and were all stray dogs to be got rid of, hydrophobia would be inevitably, if not quite, stamped out—at least very much more restricted than it is now.

With this parting advice I quite agree. Amongst the anecdotes on dogs with which Revoil concludes his book, several deserve mention, and I hope they will tickle my readers as much as they tickled me. Here is one:

Doctor Cabarras, looking out for apartments in Paris, was shown over a house by the *portier*, and they were just coming to terms when the worthy doctor, who is also a clever shot, thought it proper to inform the man that he owned a pointer.

"A dog!" exclaimed the man; "and may I ask, sir, what is your profession?"

"I am a doctor."

"Oh, all right; I will send you an answer to-night."

And the same evening there came an epistle with the following words: "We don't mind a dog in the house, oh dear no; but a doctor—never!"

Flattering for the profession, this, very. And now to

conclude. A man owns a bull-dog, with which he goes fishing—with a vengeance—in the fish-market. This is how he proceeds. He points out a healthy lobster with his stick, and asks the fishwife its price. Then he places the lobster on the ground, as if to see how lively it is.

"Oh, it is right enough," says the fishwife, "and if you don't believe it just put your nose in its claws and you will soon see. He will let you know."

"No," replies the fellow, "I won't do that, but I would not mind putting my dog's tail there."

"Well, do so then," retorts the woman. No sooner said than done.

"Come here, Plock! come here," says the master; and in a moment the lobster holds tight on the dog's caudal appendage. Of course, as soon as he is released, the dog bolts, dragging the lobster away with him at full-speed.

"Here, I say, call back your dog!" yells the woman then; "he is taking my lobster away!"

"Oh no, he is not," replies the joker; "why don't *you* call back your lobster? Anyhow, I will run after them and see."

Away he goes, and is seen no more. Presumably that identical lobster graces his table at supper-time.

There are many more veridic, and otherwise, anecdotes in the book, but I must refer my readers to the volume itself, and I warrant them a treat.

FRENCH HOUNDS.

It would be perfectly impossible to give a description of every type of hound to be met with in France, because in many cases the crosses have been made so regardless of system as to make the results anything but classifiable or pleasing types to the eye of the sportsman. Why it should have been so is easily understood. Previous to the Revolution of 1793 hounds were only to be found in the hands of princes of the blood, or very rich noblemen, who took good care to keep their respective breeds pure. Hence, up to the Revolution, the standard type of the French hounds was well defined. At the Revolution, however, a scattering of masters and hounds took place, and the masses, with the blind rage of all surexcited masses, vented their wrath even on hounds, simply because they had belonged to aristocrats! This being so, a few hounds only escaped this "doggy" St. Bartholomew, and eventually, when order was restored, the types had to be interbred, and also crossed withEnglish blood, in order to replenish the various kennels then almost, if not quite, empty. Thus, already, a certain amount of "blurring" took place; but nevertheless the large packs, to a certain extent at any rate, preserved good working hounds, if at the expense of definite types. And to this day this is the case. Where, however, small packs are kept and worse still, wherever a number of sportsmen keep only one or two hounds, then the confusion has become something awful to contemplate. Men who knew absolutely nothing of hunting or of hounds, by a series of successful commercial or professional enterprises found themselves rich or well-to-do; and as a gentleman on the Continent must, at least, make a show of being a sportsman, all *parvenus* must perforce take to keeping hounds. How they are taken in, yearly, by knowing dealers, is too well known a fact to be dwelt upon. Anything in the shape of a dog will do for these gentry, and the most astounding crosses are palmed off upon them with perfect impunity. Then some of these newly-made Nimrods take upon themselves to improve (?) their very remarkable curs, by breeding from them with those of their friends (which are equally bad), and the results, as regards hounds in the hands of private sportsmen, are, to say the least, wonderful to behold.

The lover of good hound-types must, therefore, look for them in France only in large kennels, for it is only by an extraordinary chance that he will find a true type of hound in the hands of a private sportsman. As regards harriers and beagles, however, these will be found only in private hands, and they are pretty fair; but a great deal of blind crossing is also beginning to take place there.

I will now proceed to classify the leading types, as Revoil classes them, and will also give a short description of each, as far as my experience, and a reference to leading French works, can assist me.

The *Gascon* hounds are hound-marked, very strongly built, not remarkably swift, but very steady on the scent. They are noted for their partiality for wolf-hunting. The

Count of Lecoulteux de Canteleu states in his work, "La Vénerie Française, et la Chasse du Loup," that his Gascon hounds have feet like those of a wolf. I should not be surprised if a wolf cross had caused this peculiarity, especially as several masters of hounds had, in olden times, a very strong partiality for introducing wolf-blood in their kennels. Even to the present day this intercrossing does take place, especially where fierce work has to be performed; and it is notorious that several of the lymers and hounds attached to Government packs of wolf-hounds are crossed with wolf. The Gascon hounds are, perhaps, the oldest breed in France of which authentic historical notice has been preserved. As far back as Henry IV. their praise has been sung, and in modern times great value is attached to them. They are rather obstinate, *soit dit en passant*, and will stick to their line whether right or wrong. They, however (be it said to their credit), rarely go wrong, their power of scent being very acute. Their tongue is a succession of very deep notes, not unlike distant thunder, and no doubt such a music must, to the quarry, sound pretty much like a *de profundis*. Some heavy prices have been paid for good specimens of the breed. Revoil, in his "Histoire Anecdotique des Chiens," states that M. Miramon de Montbrun prized them so much that he refused, when being short of cash, sixteen thousand francs (about six hundred and forty pounds) for a couple of his Gascon hounds.

The *chiens de Bordeaux* and the *chiens de Toulouse*, two varieties of the Gascon hounds, are remarkable for their very careful way of hunting; they are not brilliant by any means, but when once fairly on, they rarely take the change, and are always to be trusted.

The Saintonge hounds have a deal of white, with a few

flecks of tan-and-black over the limbs, and generally a light tan-and-black saddle and root of stern. They have sensible heads, with good *os occipitis*, moderately long ears, well-arched necks, stiff propellers, stout loins, good fore-legs and feet, and broad breasts. Their flag is thin, and not feathered. On the whole they do not look speedy, but they can go a cracker to a view-halloo. When hunting a difficult scent they are most careful and steady. They are getting very scarce.

Of course, both Gascony and Saintonge claim many different breeds besides those which I have described, and which are considered the true types.

The Poitevins are either hound-marked or black-and-white. Their powers of scent are notorious, so that they are essentially *the* hounds for difficult cases; but whilst acknowledging that much, yet the absurd and impossible powers of scent which by some writers and owners of kennels are attributed to them must be taken *cum grano salis*, and I am afraid with a moderately large grain. Thus the author I have just cited states in his work that these hounds will hunt readily, and unerringly, a wolf, even if he has passed *six* or *eight* hours before the hounds were uncoupled! Now, granting that the effluvia of a wolf is pretty strong, methinks the hound that can make it out at speed, six or eight hours after his passage, must be endowed with an extraordinary power of scent, and that may happen now and then with a particular specimen; but that a whole pack should exhibit this extraordinary power, is, to say the least, rather startling. The Poitevins never reached the great size of the Gascon-Saintonge hounds, I believe, because they have been interbred to such an extraordinary extent in order to preserve the breed, that, like the Laverack setters, it is rare to get a good upstanding fair-sized specimen, and the puppies are very hard to rear.

When the Poitevins are crossed, however, with Gascon or Saintongeois blood, some good hounds with substance and style are produced.

The Poitevin hounds are divided into two classes, those of the high Poitou and those of the low Poitou. The former are much prized for roebuck-shooting, and the latter for wolf-hunting. Both breeds, nowadays, are very frequently crossed with the foxhound, and, as might be readily expected, a great deal of speed is thus infused into the packs; but it is said the cross is affecting the truthfulness of their scenting powers. Perhaps so, but I doubt it, because on such strong scent as that of deer or wolf surely foxhound blood can hold its own in hunting, and go a burster withal; therefore, if anything, the cross must be all benefit to the packs.

M. Revoil mentions the blue hounds of Foudras, but they are so rare that a notice is hardly necessary. They are a cross of Gascon and Saintonge hounds.

The Ceres hounds are still rarer, and are usually red-and-white. Their tongue is not loud, but they are said to hunt remarkably well.

The Norman hounds have been so much crossed with English blood that to all intents and purposes they are foxhounds. They run very fast, carry their heads high, and take readily to any scent.

The Artois hounds have the voices of bloodhounds, and are so sure on the trail that their talents have passed into a proverb. Their markings are tricolour, or black-and-white, or harepied-and-white. For work, they will hunt anything but a fox, says Revoil; yet the same author states that they are good on wolf. If so, their dislike to "the vermin" is all but unaccountable.

The Vendée hounds are either rough or smooth. The former are usually much preferred wherever a very rough country has to be traversed; but both breeds are very highly valued, especially for wolf or boar hunting, on account of their great intrepidity, and I might add ferocity. Let a stranger beware how he meddles with them. Their markings are lemon-and-white, red-and-white, and, now and then, black-lemon-and-white (especially the rough ones), and a few are iron-gray.

These hounds are held in very high esteem on the Continent, so much so that two regular fairs are held yearly for their exclusive sale and barter. Both fairs take place at Bourbon-Vendée, the first one on the second Monday in May, and the second on the second Monday in July. At such times an immense number of French, German, and Belgian masters of hounds turn up at Bourbon-Vendée, and the prices realised are very high. Those breeders who have been fortunate enough to secure true specimens make the greater part of their income by breeding systematically for these fairs, and the speculation is invariably found to pay—and to pay well—so much is thought in France of a really well-bred and good hound.

The *griffons Vendéens* are the roughest of the breed. They are wonderfully plucky, and never give in, either to wolf or boar.

The *chiens de St. Hubert*, says Revoil, are bloodhounds, introduced, it is said, in the seventh century, in the Ardennes, by St. Hubert, from whom they take their generic name. The breed had been carefully preserved by the abbots of St. Hubert, who were great sportsmen, and at the time of the Norman conquest they were brought into England, where they are now almost exclusively to be found. Most of the lymers attached to French packs, however, are bloodhounds, more or less crossed either with the hounds they run with, or with pointer blood.

The *griffons Bretons* are large-sized hounds full of "go" and fire; they are usually marked light tan, or brindle-and-black mixed with white-and-gray. They are excellent hounds, and extremely plucky. In Brittany they are used exclusively for wolf and boar hunting, and rarely miss giving a good account of their quarry.

The *griffons de Bresse* are getting very scarce, and I cannot say that it is a pity, for they are ugly hounds, and give tongue in such a lamentable manner that there can be no great pleasure in listening to them. Joined to this, although very sure, they were very slow, and, withal, much given to "babbling" without sense, rhyme, or reason. The *chiens briquets* are hounds of a size between that of ordinary hounds and that of beagles. We would here class them as harriers. In France, however, they are used indifferently for hare, rabbit, roebuck, &c. They are of no particular breed, and are used chiefly to drive the quarry to the gun. Of course, there are two grand classes of *briquets*—those smooth (*briquets à poil ras*), and those rough (*briquets à poil dur*, or *briquets griffons*). The latter are preferred for thick under-coverts, because, owing to their short stature and thick coats, they can go anywhere, and don't mind thorns and briars.

I have seen many *briquets* at work, both smooth and rough, as almost every sportsman owns one, but I cannot say I like them; they are neither sure nor steady. Joined to that, they are as obstinate as mules, and if each of them "finds" a separate scent, they will all follow their individual quarry without obeying your calls, and so you do not know which way to go, or where to wait for a shot. I now come to the French beagles, called *Bassets*. There are three classes, those with straight legs (*à jambes droites*); those with fore-legs half crooked (*à jambes demi-torses*); finally, those with fore-legs quite crooked (*à jambes torses*). Then each of these three classes has smooth-coated and rough-coated specimens.

For work there are excellent *Bassets* of all breeds in the hands of private sportsmen. They hunt slow but sure, and with good management the shooter is about certain to bag their quarry.

ALGERIAN GREYHOUNDS.

THESE greyhounds are held in the highest esteem, and are considered as very valuable, large sums of money being frequently paid for good specimens. Their colour is generally a light brindle mousy tint, without admixture of any other colour. They are generally tall, stoutish, very powerful, and fairly fast. Their heads are rather peculiar, inasmuch that they show the *os occipitis* quite as much as many hounds; and they have, withal, an uncommonly long pair of jaws, which gives them a rather wolfy appearance. They are generally desperate fighters, and are, as a rule, very troublesome with strangers, being apt to seize any individual whose look or dress does not exactly coincide with their own opinions on the matter. And as their masters rather delight in seeing any onslaught of the sort, and tacitly or openly encourage them in such little diversions, why it is not always safe for the bare-legged beggars of the province of Algiers or Tunis to get into too close contact with these sharp-teethed customers. I bear in mind now a treat of the sort we had when we landed at Algiers (for the first time, as far as I was concerned), about eight years ago. We were "doing the Mediterranean," and, of course, *facile princeps*, Gibraltar had our first visit; its opposite neighbour, Algiers, came next in our attention, and we got there ashore early in the morning so as to see what was to be seen before the midday heat had rendered walking well-nigh impossible. Two or three vagabonds who were loafing in the sun and scowling at us, suddenly got up and began scampering away. Coming up the street was an Arab chief on his gray horse, and by his side trotted a very handsome *sloughi* (greyhound). Whether the said chief had said something or not to the dog it would be hard to say, for his countenance remained throughout perfectly imperturbable ; but anyhow the coursing we had then and there was an infinite treat to our men, who fairly roared with laughter. The way this sloughi cut after one, then the other, and then the third of these beggars, and gave a wrench here and a wrench there, was, to say the least, very suggestive. In a moment the place was cleared and the dog went back to his master, who looked as serious as ever ; but I strongly suspect that in his innermost soul he was delighted. All sloughis are marked by their owners with a star on the forehead ; why I cannot tell—a mere custom, I presume. It is also said that their fore-legs are occasionally fired to give strength to the articulation.* Why the Arabs are so fond of their greyhounds, however, is very easily explained. First of all, since their many periodical insurrections, by which they have repeatedly tried to set the French authorities at defiance, the French have found it expedient to forbid the sale of gunpowder to the tribes, for fear they should use that powder against themselves. This being the case, any Arab who has sporting tendencies must either resort to some device in order to procure gunpowder, or, failing in getting any, he must

* See General Daumas's book on the Desert.

sport without. But sport he shall, for the love of sport is in him a second nature. He would decidedly prefer using a gun. The noise of the explosion, the flash of the flame, the smell of gunpowder, are all very dear to his soul; but if he cannot get the precious compound, his dog and his hawk will amply supply his needs. Not that he cares much himself for game; mutton is his favourite dish on gala-days; but when away in the wilderness he likes to pick up whatever game he finds, or, if near a town, he kills birds and hares for the markets; for I need not state that the European residents have naturally caused a very great demand for anything of the sort.

Now, a good sloughi experiences no difficulty whatsoever in keeping his master and family in great comparative comfort. The price of a hare will keep them all for a week; so no wonder the Arab prizes the clever sloughi, who never or rarely misses his quarry. Of course it will readily be understood that there is no question about fair coursing in such proceedings. A hare is found, let the greyhound kill it and bring it back, and he is a good greyhound; let him miss it and miss killing others, and his own fate will be pretty clear. In short it is merely a question of market. Most Algerian greyhounds hunt for their own game, and have a very fair amount of scenting powers. They are, to tell the truth, likely to own this last property all to themselves, for although the British officers garrisoned at Gibraltar, and the French officers who reside in Algeria, have repeatedly imported pointers, setters, and spaniels into the Algerian territory, it has always been found that eventually these dogs lost their scenting faculties to an alarming extent, and their offspring are almost invariably noseless. Therefore the sloughi is likely to be the only canine assistant to be relied upon, and he thrives on the terrific heat which dulls his European cousins' faculties.

The Algerian greyhound, like ours, is very "tender." As soon as winter weather draws nigh he is wrapped up in his clothing, and the greatest care is paid him; in fact throughout his life he is regularly made a tremendous pet of. It is not unusual, by any means, to see very young puppies nursed by the women as though they were babies, and sharing with the babies in all their privileges. Should a sloughi bitch die when giving birth to her litter, the youngsters are at once handed over to the care of the women, who rarely fail to give a very good account of their charges. When a good dog has achieved a reputation, the owners of bitches flock to his master from hundreds of miles for the dog's services, pretty much as is done within the shores of the "tight little island;" but in the desert the journeys have to be performed on horseback, and a great deal of time and trouble have necessarily to be taken to ensure a desirable crossing. Such is the horror of Arabs for any low admixture of cur blood, that they sometimes kill the bitches that have granted their favours to sheep-dogs and other breeds, or, if they spare her life, her progeny is doomed. When, however, the connection is known to have been of the desirable sort, many are the applications made for puppies even before the puppies are born. When three or four months old the youngsters are made to race after and kill rats. When five or six months old they are entered to hares; but it is only when fully a year old that they are slipped at gazelles, and then, according to General Daumas, only at young ones, so as not to exhaust the dogs. It is only when fully developed that they are brought to course full-grown gazelles. The way in which the latter sport is carried out is simple enough. The dog is secured by a leash, and hunts the scent like a lymer. When the gazelles are discovered the master slips his dog, who thereupon chooses amongst the herd a particular animal, to which he devotes his attention, generally with success if he is up to the mark; but it does really take some running to secure a three-year-old gazelle, so generally the greyhound runs cunning until he gets near enough for a rush, when he puts on all steam and springs on his quarry. For hares no precautions, such as putting the dogs in slips, are taken. The Arab, either on horseback or on foot, accompanies the dogs, who are loose, and he beats the ground whilst they hunt about for scent. As soon as a hare is started, at her the sloughis go, and, of course, she is soon collared.

These greyhounds are also employed for partridge-hawking. The sportsman carries his hawk on his turban, and when the greyhounds flush a bird, or a covey, away sails the hawk after them, and soon secures one. Formerly, however, only the chiefs of tribes kept either hawks or greyhounds. It would have been then considered perfectly ridiculous for any man but one of gentle blood to own either. No matter whether rich or poor, the chief was, almost by his birthright, entitled to such companions in the chase; but no matter how well off a commoner might have been, he would have been laughed at and derided by his tribe-fellows if he had had the impudence to take to grey-hounds and hawks. Now, however, things have altered. Since the conquest of Algeria by the French, many of the chiefs have lost their authority, and not a few have been killed. Then French manners told on the old notions, and now anyone who can afford it may keep either a sloughi or a hawk, or both, with, however, this distinction, that the well-to-do Arab keeps them for sport, whereas his poorer brethren resort to them simply as means of subsistence. No wonder then that such a value is set upon the Algerian greyhound! When a sloughi dies, General Daumas tells us that it is, for its master's family, the greatest calamity that could possibly affect it, since he literally earned their daily bread. In the ordinary routine of life the dog is treated as well as the head of the family himself, being fed on the best that the resources of the tent can procure; and he sleeps, usually, by the side of his master, sharing the same couch. These dogs' affection for their masters is quite touching. Some die of grief if their master remains away for any length of time, and all pine away from the moment they are separated from him. On his return, however, the wildest joy prevails in the household, and it is not rare for the sloughi to spring on his master's saddle for his caresses. Very many of these greyhounds wear ornaments of all kinds round their necks; and some of these fancy collars, when the dogs belong to rich men, are very valuable, whereas the sloughi who belongs to a poor man is adorned in a rough-and-ready fashion with common shells, strung together on a bit of common twine. In short, no matter who owns him, the sloughi is pretty sure to be very well treated. This is all the more curious that all other breeds of dogs are invariably looked upon with contempt by the Arabs. They cannot rank a pointer or a setter, for instance, with their sloughis. They have not the sense to. They do not understand the subtlety of a dog standing to his point, and being backed by his companion. They only admire a display of speed, because it appeals to their eyes without fatiguing themselves, hence the great adoration which they pay to the sloughis. The dog that can catch is *the* dog, by excellence, for them, and no doubt they are quite right in their way; for of what earthly use would a pointer or a setter be to men who cannot shoot, either flying or running? As a matter of fact, most Arabs, when accompanying Europeans as guides, are wonderfully struck by the work of the pagans' dogs; but they preserve a very stolid countenance, and only among themselves do they discuss the performance, and, whilst admitting the admirable fashion in which their French or English employers manage their sport, yet they invariably conclude their discussion by the exclamation, "It is all very well, but give us a good sloughi, and then we want no gun, and no powder and shot to secure our game!" Of course, as far as that goes, it is right enough from their point of view.

Some sloughis belonging to poachers are, however, trained to half-point at game, when their masters, if they own guns, pot the game on the ground, and, if they have no guns, they knock the hares on the heads in their forms with clubs; or, when partridges are flushed, they throw, in the "brown" of the covey, a short heavy stick, which rarely fails to bring down to mother earth a few of the feathered tribe. That it takes a good deal of practice to be successful in any undertaking of the sort many sportsmen will admit readily, but that it is being done by many of these men as their daily avocation is well known to European residents in Algeria, and a visit to the markets on any day will convince the most sceptical. Almost all the birds brought there will show, as plain as could be, marks of the sticks by their smashed heads and broken wings, but no gunshot will be found in them. As for the hares, they are either caught by the sloughis, or smashed with clubs by the sloughis' owners ; and not one hare in a thousand will show traces of shot, that is when they come from the tribes, for now and then a European finds too much of his game on his hands, and sells it, in which case of course every head of it has been duly shot.

Some of the European residents have, of late, imported greyhounds of their own, or procured some sloughis, and a good deal of coursing now takes place in the neighbourhood of all large towns, wherever consulates or large stations are established. Thus many of the French officers garrisoned at Algiers are to be seen with their British *confrères* from the other shore, now and then, cavalcading about in the country in search of a little excitement with their swift dogs; but gazelles are only to be found now in the desert, and one must ride many wearisome miles to indulge in the sport.

Wild boars are also roused by sloughis, but the dogs have only to harass them and drive them out. They could not kill the boars. The Arabs, however, despise boars. To them they are *unclean* animals, and when they kill one they never touch it, but allow it to rot away where it fell, and carnivora and birds of prey are welcome to make a meal of it.

To resume, then, the sloughi, or Algerian greyhound, is essentially *the* sporting dog for Algeria. None other is acknowledged by the native population, and he (the sloughi), when good, is looked upon there almost as a demigod.

PARADING PRIZE DOGS.

IF the duty of a writer be to make himself at all times the organ of public opinion, in the performance of that duty I think I will get the thanks of the public for drawing attention to a much-needed improvement in connection with dog-shows. I refer to parading, which does not exist at dog-shows, and which, if adopted, would enable the public to decide for themselves whether the judges have, in their adjudication of the awards, done their duty well. At all horse-shows nowadays the parade of winners is looked forward to by the public as the time for comparing notes and analysing the decisions arrived at, and it is a most satisfactory arrangement. No one can judge of the qualities of a horse if he only sees it in its stall or stable. The very crudest recruit in horseflesh will need seeing the animal "out" before he pronounces on its merits; and yet, as regards dogs, the public have to see them on their benches, and the visitors have to draw on their imagination and picture to themselves the winners as they should be, in their respective degrees of perfection, without being able to refer to their own eyes for some confirmatory evidence of the awards that have been made, unless they are present throughout during the judging. Now it is obvious that the vast majority of people cannot afford to remain a whole day watching the judging, however interesting this process may appear to those pecuniarily or otherwise interested in the awards. Moreover, this could be done only when a single judge was officiating; but where several judges are at the same time at work in several different rings, it is self-evident that, as the critic cannot be in several places at the same time, he cannot therefore see what takes place; and as to his judging from the dogs on their benches whether the awards have been properly made or not, it is simply nonsense—he cannot do it. You may look at a dog who is lying down on his bench as much as you like, you can't see his points. If you are a stranger, and try to rouse him, he is as likely as not inclined to bite you. Some show dogs are extremely queer dogs to deal with. They have been lifted up bodily so often that it makes them quake again to see you come near them. Some people poke them in the ribs with their umbrellas to make them get up, and that is not calculated to improve their tempers if they are peacefully inclined. So that, taken all in all, when once a dog is brought back on his bench, there is no knowing what he is like to any certainty. He may show himself well there at times, but if he does so it is only for a moment, and that is all. The majority of show dogs, when once released from duty, put themselves down in all sorts of positions and shapes, and Heaven knows what they do with their points then. Sometimes an attendant will take a dog out and show him, but show attendants are not supposed to do that much; and, as a rule, they are chary of doing it, unless they see prospectively an immediate result—*i.e.* a fee.

Therefore I contend that the general public do not see half the sights which dog-shows ought to afford them; and I certainly think that, if a certain hour were to be fixed upon at dog-shows for parading the prize dogs, people would flock there to see the procession, and that it would also prove the severest criticism of the proper awarding of prizes that could be devised, simply for this reason, that, as matters now stand, almost every unsuccessful exhibitor may "kick up a shindy" if he likes; no one cares a straw about his grumbling; but supposing the said grumbler, when the parade took place, took the opportunity of pointing out his wrongs; then I venture to say that that man would soon find redress in public opinion; and, after all, public opinion is the main test of everything. Yes, I am convinced that if a general parade of the prize-winners, class after class, in catalogue order, were to take place at every dog-show as soon as the judging was over—I am convinced, I repeat, that it would put a stop to favouritism, if there be any, which I do not doubt; to ignorance on the part of some judges, which sometimes is glaringly patent; and, finally, that it would place the awards made at dog-shows on such a footing as no private clamour could ever dislodge it from, and that would be a very desirable end to attain. And why should it not be done? Of course this leading out of prize-winners would entail a little extra exertion on the part of the attendants; but this, after all, would not be much, and could not compare with the trouble inherent to showing off prize horses, for instance. The latter have to be saddled and bridled, or else put in harness, &c., for that sort of thing, whereas a dog is always ready to be brought out; and people who have taken prizes ought not to begrudge showing to the public (who pays for everything) what they took their prizes with; at least, "them is my sentiments" on the point, as Mr. Micawber has it. But if anybody, or several "bodies," should differ from me, I hope they will not call me names, because that would not prove that I am wrong.

WOLF-SHOOTING IN FRANCE.

THOSE in search of a little excitement would do well to pack up their guns and go to France for some wolf-hunting. Since the war of 1870 wolves have so increased (says *L'Acclimatation*) in the southern and midland provinces, that the official *louvetiers* are seemingly unable to cope with their numbers, and a new bill is being brought before the Government to authorise every means of destruction being resorted to by the country folks. Poisoning, however, will be restricted by the usual laws; but shooting, with or without a license, will be allowed whenever and wherever wolves will be concerned. In short, all the year round, shooters will not only be allowed to wage war against the daring depredators, but actually the official rewards for their destruction will be increased. Thus every she-wolf in cub will be worth a reward of 100f. (£4) to the man who succeeds in killing her. For an ordinary wolf, 80f. (£3 4s.) will be paid; for a cub, 40f. (£1 12s.); and an extraordinary reward of 150f. (£6) will be paid to anyone killing any wolf proved to have attacked and bitten women and children. I would suggest to those fond of that sort of sport to take over with them a couple or two of large foxhounds with a temper, if possible, and I will warrant they will have good sport with the wolves.

FRENCH OFFICIAL WOLF-HOUNDS.

(*Équipages de Louveterie.*)

I.

WERE it not for the extreme preserving of ground game which goes on in some parts of the land, our tight little island ought to be well-nigh considered a very paradise for farmers, for here they have at least no large game or carnivora to contend against, as their brethren of France have; and I have often heard the latter exclaim how they wished their lot had been cast on this side of the Channel, when I told them how England, Scotland, and Ireland had been thoroughly cleared of wild-boars and wolves, and how deer and roebuck were kept in suitable quarters, where they were made to pay and show sport, and did no appreciable mischief.

"But you hunt foxes," they would add, "and of course preserve them. This being so, what about the damage they commit?"

"Oh, that is paid for by the poultry-fund."

"Ah, we wish somebody would start here a wheat-fund, for the wheat wild-boars, stags, and roebucks do eat and spoil! and a sheep-fund, for the sheep and lambs which the wolves do levy upon our flocks whenever they have a chance!"

Yes, it cannot be denied that these men have to put up with a great deal; and as farming is, as a rule, carried on in France by small capitalists, the losses tell heavily on each individual, whereas a man of substance might perhaps put up with it with more resignation. But imagine the feelings of the man who has only one field of standing wheat, and finds it in the morning as thoroughly wrecked and spoiled as if a squadron of cavalry had effected a charge through it; or picture the wailings of the poor Vendéen or Breton peasant who finds his crop of chestnuts gone and his maize torn up by the roots by wild-boars, or one of his *two* or *three* sheep gone for ever, carried away by a wolf!

The despair of the poor family may better be imagined than described; and were it not for the organisation of regular packs of hounds, bred and kept purposely for the work of destroying all obnoxious animals, there is not the slightest doubt that the rural populations of the wildest districts would simply be starved to death by these depredators.

Government in France takes the supreme direction in these matters. Noblemen fond of hunting (as all noblemen are or ought to be) are nominated captains or lieutenants of *louveterie*, and every assistance is given them in the furtherance of their office, which is *primâ facie*, as their title indicates, the destruction of wolves; but they also go in for wild-boars, roebuck, and deer whenever these get so numerous as to become a nuisance. The institution of these *louveteries* is admirably organised, it is also admirably managed, and the peasants fairly worship the captain or lieutenant of the district; and they may well say that, "after Heaven's help, all they can possibly reap or keep depends upon this officer's protection."

A regular wolf-hunting establishment under official sanction is bound to attend as soon as convenient to all complaints sent in by the farmers and peasants; but it is left to the discretion of the master to actually carry out the work of destruction. This at first sight may appear strange, but it must be borne in mind that the peasants are occasionally more frightened than hurt, and not a few of them are ready to call out before they are harmed. Then there are others among them who, knowing full well that while the hounds will be drawing the woods there will be many chances of getting hares and other game, on the off-chance of thus making surreptitiously a good bag, they send bitter recriminations to the *louvetier* on the slightest pretence. That officer, however, born and bred among them, knows their ways, and when he has good grounds for believing their statements to be either unfounded or at least greatly exaggerated, he contents himself with sending word that he will attend to the business shortly. What makes this virtual pooh-poohing on his part appear to me all the more correct is the fact that anyone who likes not only may kill a wolf in any way he chooses, but also gets a monetary reward from Government for having done so. Such being the case, and very few indeed of the peasants being without guns (old army muskets or fowling-pieces), it seems strange they should prefer applying to the *louvetier* for the destruction of the marauder; and the real motive for their doing so is, as I have stated, that they wish, under covert of the official proceedings, to bag whatever they can floor; and anyone who has ever joined an equipage of wolf-hounds will testify to the fact that the number of shots that are fired in every possible direction whilst the hunting is being carried on would be totally inexplicable were it not for the fact that many animals and birds besides the hunted wolf get on the move the moment the hounds open, and these birds and animals are at once "potted."

"How is it that so many wolves are to be found about?" someone may inquire, and possibly add: "Why don't they kill the lot?"

Well, a glance at the map will show that Europe and Asia form but one continent, many parts of which are perfect deserts, where man never or rarely appears. These spots are regular warrens for the breeding of wild animals. In southern Russia alone hundreds of miles of ground are covered with impenetrable forests. Poland, Austria, Bavaria, some parts of Germany, and the Ardennes in France, besides many other spots too numerous to mention, contain strongholds which are practically inaccessible to man for hunting. In these strongholds the wolves, boars, and other beasts of the chase increase and multiply, and when comes the "loving" season they disperse themselves in couples, as they can no longer agree near others of the same breeds. Or again, when the weather gets very severe, and these animals are sorely pressed by hunger, they wander away from their then bare fastnesses, and invade those cultivated portions of the land where they may find food. Thus by reason of the, to them, two most powerful influences—love and hunger—periodical incursions of these wild animals do take place all over the land. Nothing short of wholesale extermination could prevent these incursions, and wholesale extermination is an impossibility.

It has been done in England, it is true; but what is England in extent when compared with the Continent. And again, in England, when once the stock had been destroyed, there was an end to the vermin; precisely because the tight island is an island, and wild-boars or wolves could not swim twenty odd miles of sea (at the nearest point) even if they had compasses and charts to know where they would be going. Hence, the absolute immunity enjoyed now in England from the attacks of these depredators.

Now since the whole breed cannot be put an end to on the Continent, the next best thing to be done is to keep them in check, and this the official *louvetiers* undertake to do.

Some packs of wolf-hounds are rather short-handed. It is not rare to see only four, five, or six couples of hounds uncoupled, whereas in other districts ten couples sometimes are at work, and occasionally there are more. These hounds are generally very powerfully built. Not that it requires a particularly powerful hound to hunt a wolf (I have myself shot half-a-dozen that were hunted by eleven dachshunds, and I have actually shot two others that were hunted by a single basset; the latter is an extraordinary occurrence, by-the-way); but, in order to provide against emergencies, the bigger hounds are far preferable, because they can among them despatch the wolf when they run him down; whereas with the smaller breeds the gun and the hunting-knife must come into play at once. No amount of dachshunds or bassets could kill a wolf; but he could kill or maim any amount of dachshunds and bassets, for his strength of jaw is simply prodigious. I had heard a good many tales about what wolves could do, and I used to smile. But when I saw one with my own eyes carrying a Brittany sheep in his mouth as easily as a cat would carry a mouse, I began to think that the tales might not have been quite so very Arabian after all; and when I saw two or three powerful hounds put *hors de combat* in as many bites by the same beast, I bethought myself that his grip must have been a caution. When he was killed I examined him, and found his incisors more than double the length and thickness of those of our strongest hound, which explained the severity of his bites; and his shoulders were so near his head that practically they bore the weight of whatever he carried in his mouth, the neck being extremely short. Hence the remarkable strength these animals display, and the desirability of having hounds in sufficient numbers and of sufficient size to cope against them. Moreover, the *louvetiers* generally carry a short carbine, and they wear on their hip a short and sharp *couteau de chasse*, with which to go to the rescue of their pack when occasion requires. I have never seen this hunting-knife used myself, although I observe in "Wild Sports in Brittany"* that the author saw a captain of *louvetiers* several times cutting down boars at bay, &c. It must be very ticklish work indeed. The guns of the peasants, however, and the official carbines are generally resorted to. The former are, to tell the truth, as dangerous to the hounds and to the sportsmen as they are to the wolves or wild-boars, owing to the extraordinary recklessness with which the Bretons and the Vendéens fire their weapons into the "thick." By-the-way, these peasants rarely fire single bullets. They load with what they are pleased to call *balles mariées* (wedded bullets). The long and short of this expression means simply that two ordinary

* Chapman and Hall, publishers.

bullets are flattened on one side and there soldered together, or else a piece of brass or a nail is driven forcibly through both bullets. Whichever way the affair is concocted the wounds produced by these missiles are simply awful. Somehow, coming out of the old smooth-bore army muskets, these *balles mariées* seem to gyrate as they go, and where they *do* enter the body of the beast, they make a hole as large as an ordinary ink-pot. The *louvetiers* themselves fire ordinary bullets as a very general rule ; there are, however, some exceptions. Slugs are sometimes resorted to by the foresters, but that is a mistake. Slugs fired beyond thirty yards at a wolf, even when he is running parallel to the shooter, produce absolutely no effect ; perhaps one may enter the skin, but the rest cannot pierce it. That will give an idea of the toughness of the beast. And as for boars, slugs only make them go all the faster when fired beyond that range.

Concerning, however, the latter, it must be remembered that although they are, like the wolves, tracked and killed anyhow when they become troublesome, the State offers no reward for their destruction, simply because their meat is considered ample pay for the trouble taken and the powder and shot expended. With wolves it is a different matter. Their flesh is unpalatable; and although their skins are tanned or stuffed and used either as natural history specimens or as hearthrugs or mats, and thereby some compensation may be realised by the man who destroys them, yet such is the desirability of ridding the country of them with all speed that Government pays rewards, according to a certain rate, to all successful wolf-killers. The huntsmen and whips of all the *équipages de louveterie* get the money for all the wolves killed by their hounds or by themselves, or by anyone else firing whilst their hounds are running. That is the law. But should any private individual out by himself kill a wolf, if he cuts off the head and takes it to the prefecture of the department, or to the mayor of his village, who will thereupon grant him a certificate to that effect, on presentation of this certificate to the prefecture, the shooter can cash the official reward. No license is required for shooting them, and by day or by night war may be waged against them.

In the case of a wolf having been disposed of by an *équipage de louveterie*, a certificate to that effect, granted by the captain or lieutenant of the pack to his men, ensures payment of the reward at the prefecture.

FRENCH OFFICIAL WOLF-HOUNDS.

II.

THE hounds used by the official *louvetiers* are not what we would call a "level lot" for size; moreover, they are marked in various styles, and have different coats, according to the sort of country they have to hunt, and also sometimes the whims of their individual masters. I have seen two packs at work, one in Vendée and one in Brittany. Both packs were wire-haired almost (*poils durs*), and their markings were various. Some were iron-gray and fawn, some red-and-white, others tan-and-white, others black-and-white, and some black-and-tan. Their ears are never rounded there, the masters and their men arguing, with some truth, that their long ears protect their necks from thorns, briars, &c. It certainly at any rate makes the hounds look very noble indeed, and many of them are essentially what the French hunting-men delight in having their hounds—viz. *bien coiffés* (*i.e.* with long ears, well set). These official hounds are, however, invariably good workers. Their rough coats stand them in good stead when they are thrown in the extraordinary rough coverts of Brittany and Vendée; and for this sort of work they truly need having *le poil dur*. In the more southern provinces, where the ground and forests are more comeatable, the wolf-hounds are bred smoother; but I, for one, would back the rough Vendéens and Bretons against any others for real sterling work. They have very deep tongues, and one can hear a pack miles away, when they are in full swing.

When entering puppies for any official *louveterie*, a good many recruits are usually drafted for want of pluck. For be it known to the uninitiated, that very few hounds (or dogs of any sort, in fact) take kindly to wolf-scent. The moment a youngster comes near the spot where the wild beast has passed, he puts up his bristles and carefully folds his flag under his belly. He growls then, half in fear and half in anger, and generally rushes between his master's legs for protection against the (to his mind) very imminent danger.

But some well-bred puppies take to the scent readily, and will follow the leaders without much, if any, hesitation. Such young hounds are greatly prized; others are much slower in making up their minds; but eventually they do take to wolf-hunting, whereas others never will do it. They will follow wild-boar, roebuck, or deer, but the moment they cross a wolf's track their pluck oozes out. A good wolf-hound, on the contrary, will leave any other scent for that of the wolf. There seems to be in him a rooted antipathy to the vermin, and the sportsman who has not seen a pack " giving " on a wolf has yet a treat in store. The hounds have there a foe worthy of their steel. A fox has no chance whatever when once collared, but a wolf is an immensely powerful beast, and fights to the last, and he is sure to kill or maim three or four hounds perhaps before giving up the ghost, unless a well-directed bullet puts an end to the conflict. Now it stands to reason that hounds that are used for such rough work, and still rougher battles, must needs in time become slightly ticklish, and I may state that I have never yet seen any good wolf-hound belonging to a *louveterie* that would allow me or any stranger to touch him, or even to get near him. Among themselves, unless well looked after and at once separated, they fight like very fiends; and should you ever, reader, some fine morning when journeying in the north of France, come across a pack of large grizzly hounds, scarred over the face, neck, and chest, and looking altogether like the veterans of a hundred Waterloos, you need ask no questions, they are wolf-hounds, on the trot for a draw ; and you may make up your mind that a more resolute, dare-devil, reckless lot you have never seen before anywhere, no matter where. Give them a wide berth, and, in consideration of their invincible courage, make allowance for the infirmity of their temper.

A very curious experiment in breeding wolf-hounds was tried some twenty years ago by a Breton *officier de louveterie*, who introduced actually wolf-blood into his kennel. The direct crosses, however, did not exactly answer, inasmuch that the hounds thus bred hunted and ran mute, exactly like wolves. On the other hand, they had extraordinary powers of scent, were wonderfully plucky, and had no end of bottom ; moreover, they took to wolf-hunting as readily as ducklings take to water. For tracking, running down, and for the final fight, there could have been no better hounds, but as they never gave tongue, these first crosses had to be still further hound-crossed, until the produce ran like the rest of the pack. This wolf-breeding must, to some extent, account for the ferocity of some of the members of the packs. There is in reality no such thing as a standard breed of wolf-hounds. Any hound, no matter whether a Poitevin, an Angevin, a Vendéen, or a Breton, pure or cross-bred, smooth or rough-coated (*poil fin* or *poil dur*), a large foxhound with a temper, or an otter-hound of the large breeds, provided he takes to hunting wolf, can go the pace, has a good tongue, does not mind a rough country, and is pleased with a tussle at short notice, will do, and will be enlisted readily in an equipage of *louveterie*. The officers are always on the lookout for an infusion of good bold blood, and not a few of them continually interchange those stallions and brood-bitches of theirs which have distinguished themselves in the field.

I now come to the way in which these hounds are worked.

Information having been given to the district captain or *lieutenant de louveterie* that two or three wolves are in a certain covert, he comes overnight with the pack, and draws the covert early in the morning, just as he would for any other animal. Meanwhile the peasants station themselves with their guns in such passes as they fancy the wolf may choose to take when breaking covert. Of course they nail him if they can. If not, the hounds hunt him until he comes to a standstill, when they kill him themselves, or the *louvetier*, his friends, or his *piqueurs* fire at him, or run him through with spears or *couteaux de chasse*.

If only one wolf has been complained of, it is usual for one of the whips to try overnight, with a lymer, to make out if he has not left the district, and the hounds are then taken the next morning to the spot where the *piqueur* has found the freshest "marks," when the same hunting and killing takes place.

As sport the whole affair is simply unrivalled. Wolf-hunting is essentially *bonâ-fide* hunting. There is no wild riding to be indulged in there, for the riding is generally of the roughest description, and the hounds must hunt every inch of the way. The wolf occasionally takes it into his head to make a clear bolt, and he will run twenty leagues sometimes, right away into another country, that is if he can break covert. If, however, when trying to do so he scents or sees one of the shooters in ambush, he remains in the vast covert, and rings his changes with a vengeance, but is bound eventually to come to grief, unless he succeeds in running the hounds into darkness. The music of the hounds, and general "go" of that sort of hunting is grand in the extreme, and as regards the kill it is simply "hell let loose," and it makes one's hair stand on end to hear and to see the worry.

The *louvetiers* have a regular set of hunting "calls," which they play on their enormous *cors de chasse*. Thus there are the find, the *bien aller* (*i.e.* all going well); *la vue* (*i.e.* catching sight); *le loup* (*i.e.* the wolf); *les animaux en compagnie* (*i.e.* several wolves running together); and *la mort* (the death); all distinct, soul-stirring, and far-sounding fanfares, which apprise the dispersed field of what is taking place with the hounds. There is a good deal of ceremonial observed, be it remarked, throughout the hunt; and a stranger will be very favourably impressed by the excellent order and discipline which are invariably maintained. Extreme courtesy is universally shown to foreigners joining the sport; so any gentleman who would like to see it carried out need have no hesitation whatever as to what his reception would be. The moment he joins the *officier de louveterie*, the latter takes him, so to speak, under his particular protection, and will take care to show him the very cream of the sport.

Concerning the hunting fanfares, the tyro wishing to join in the fray, if he has a slight knowledge of music, will do well to study them, so as to know their particular meaning when he hears them. He will find them given at full length in the "Traité de Vénerie," par De Yauville, 1859. Forty-two fanfares are written therein, and it contains, moreover, a good deal of useful information about continental hunting. There are other treatises which I can also recommend to the hunting student, such as "La Chasse aux Chiens Courants," par Le Verrier de la Couterie; "La Chasse Royale," par Robert de Salnove; "La Chasse à Courre et à Tir," par Le Baron de Lage de Chaillon, A. de la Rue, and the Marquis de Cherville; &c.

In conclusion, let me hint to sportsmen that wolf-hunting as carried on by the official French *équipages de louveterie*, is a thing never to be forgotten when once seen, and that a more manly, daring, and soul-stirring sport does not exist in the annals of any land. It is throughout a mixture of scientific hunting, clever riding under difficulties, and a spice of danger—the latter an element which is sure to recommend it to the average British hunting-man.

CONTINENTAL POINTERS AND SETTERS.

It cannot be denied that there are some nicely-bred pointers and setters in Germany, Belgium, and France; but it must also be admitted that there are there some very "queer" specimens indeed, and were Mr. R. Ll. Price to see face to face some of the German, French, or Belgian so-called braques, or should Mr. Purcell Llewellin chance to meet with a French covert or marsh griffon, I am afraid both these connoisseurs would decline *in toto* tracing any pointer or setter blood in the respective specimens placed before them. Yet admire the power of patience! These braques and griffons, through sheer long training, are brought to do (pretty fairly) the work that is expected of them by their peculiar owners. To be candid, I was myself very sorely puzzled on sundry occasions when similar sorry specimens were introduced to my notice.

"You want a good marsh setter, sir," said a Belgian professional shooter to me once. "Well, sir, I know a good one—a griffon, and he will suit you."

"A griffon?" I said, musingly; "what is a griffon?" And in my innermost soul I connected the forthcoming griffon with the mythological hippogriph. I was not so far wrong after all, for the aforementioned griffon turned out to be a most extraordinary nondescript, a cross between a cocoa-nut mat and a large poodle to all appearances. But oh, wonder of wonders! he was, there is no denying it, a capital marsh setter, but (and that is where the absence of purity in the breed strongly asserted itself) he was fully seven or eight years old, had been since his puppyhood in the breaker's hands, and was *just beginning to point!* So, ye valiant breeders of thoroughbreds, who travel hundreds, nay thousands of miles, yearly, in visits to shows, to trials, to private kennels, and who spare no trouble and expense in getting the best of every breed, take heart of grace, and congratulate yourselves that your exertions are not altogether ill-requited, since *your* specimens of *your* respective breeds take to pointing almost without tuition at, not seven years of age, but seven months not uncommonly, and I do not by any means despair of seeing eventually youthful pointers and setters getting on their points in a workmanlike manner at seven weeks old. Should our actual breeders' care be transmitted to our posterity, some of the dogs of the future will probably point from their canine cradle. Could anything point to a more vicious state of things in breeding matters than the fact that a dog, well worked for five or six seasons, yet only began to do his work in his seventh year?

But now the question arises—why are such dogs used? For a very excellent reason—there are no others to be had, comparatively speaking. Good specimens are scattered wide, here and there, and those who own them stick to them, and will not allow them to cross.

There are on the Continent four recognised classes for

setting dogs, viz. the braque, the épagneul, the griffon, and the barbet.

As I have for the last fifteen years shot in the fields, marshes, and woods of France, Germany, and Belgium, whenever I have had the opportunity of going abroad, I have seen all the breeds of dogs at work, and I feel that I can speak with confidence about their points and characteristics.

The generic term *braques* includes all pointing and setting dogs with short hair, such as English pointers and Spanish pointers, as well as the original French braques, of which there are no less than six grand varieties—viz. the *braque Dupuy*, the *braque de Picardie*, and those of Navarre, of Anjou, of Allemagne, and *Du Bourbonnais*. Concerning the English pointer, the opinion of many continental shooters is that he is too fast for their narrow fields, and that he is totally unsuited to the requirements of the man who wants a dog-of-all-work. Of course few pointers will take kindly to their pot-hunting style; that is clear, if that is what they mean. To wish that a thoroughbred pointer should go hunting in thick and prickly covert, through furze after rabbits, and to expect him to retrieve from land and water, *in all weathers*, is too much of a joke for some of the dogs' feelings.

Hence the soft and thin-skinned English pointer is held in mediocre esteem by any but the rich shooters, who like to have a well-bred, elegant-looking dog anyhow for a companion.

In the provinces, when the land is open, however, the English pointer is preferred, because he saves the sportsmen's legs considerably, can go at a good pace, and being in a plain his master can always see him. Of course, as time goes on matters will improve, and a certain proof that the pointer blood, at any rate, is favourably looked upon is that almost invariably the services at stud of a good British pointer, who works well in the field, are always eagerly sought after everywhere on the Continent.

The Spanish pointer is a slow coach, and a heavy one withal; but if he is slow he is sure, and he possesses a nose which some English pointers might very well envy. The style of the Spanish gentleman is pretty much like that of his master—*i.e.* he takes matters very coolly, never is in a hurry, trots along in earnest, but without any flurry, is everlasting in bottom if not pressed, and dearly loves the gun; in short, he hunts *for* the gun, whereas the English pointer hunts for himself. A good Spaniard will come to a point with the stanchness of an Egyptian pyramid. There is no nonsense about *him*. The birds are there, and no mistake. I never saw a Spanish pointer making a deliberate false point. In short, he uses his good sense, and when coming on a scent, he does not get cataleptic for good, unless he makes sure that they are there still. If the birds lie well, the Spanish pointer moves his nose in their individual direction, where they are scattered, so that, within half-a-dozen or so, one may get a tolerable idea of the numerical force of the covey. Some dogs are very apt to do that sort of thing when they are old and experienced, and I strongly opine (especially when they take their point by dropping) that they have been much used by netting poachers. Given a quiet moonlight night, and good fields with plenty of birds, and a Spanish pointer well trained to the work and two poachers will "drag" hundreds of partridges in the night. But the dog must lie down on his point, not necessarily when taking his point, but when he sees the men coming, or when the net gets over him.

There is an enormous amount of game taken in that manner on the Continent, and were it not for the sagacity of their dogs, it would be a very difficult matter indeed for the men to know exactly where to drop their abominable implements.

Hence the Spanish pointer being a steady ranger, perfect finder, and strict pointer, is almost universally adopted by poachers wherever quiet work has to be undertaken by them. The best Spanish pointers I have ever seen have, almost invariably, been purchased by sportsmen directly from poachers, and I must say that where game was pretty plentiful no better allies to the gun were needed. Had there been a deal of ground to cover, matters would have been different, however, for the English pointer will indubitably cover ten times more ground in the same time than his Spanish *confrère*.

The *braque Dupuy* is very much like the English pointer in build, but his head is squarer, and he is stouter on his pins. He is a moderately fast ranger, and a clever finder of game, very stanch and steady. When brought up to it he does not mind rough work, but few of them go well to water. They have rather peculiar heads, the muzzle being very short and square, the nose turning up slightly, their ears are set high, and they have plenty of dew-lap. They are dashing workers, and are very greatly prized.

I have seen a brace that would come to their points at awful distances, by a tropical heat; hence, for the hot departments of France they are admirably suited. The braques of Picardy, Navarre, and Anjou differ only in markings.

Some so-called German pointers are, however, perfect monsters in size. I have seen one which was as big as a small donkey. When this fellow came past you at a trot he shook the very ground, at least I used to say so to his owner. I only saw that dog twice out in the field, and never saw him on point. He seemed to have no nose, although his master greatly prized him, perhaps merely for the originality of his size. He retrieved fur, however, very well, bringing a hare or a rabbit a quarter of a mile, if necessary; but as he swallowed two or three partridges, I voted him rather *de trop*, and begged to be excused killing game to such a brute. On the other hand, I have seen some pointers in Germany (not to be confused with German pointers) which were excellent in their way; but then again, tastes differ. A German shooter expects his pointer to point everything, and to remain steady until the gun can get near, in the open. But under covert the dog is expected to spring roebucks, hares, and rabbits, and *mirabile dictu, he must give tongue* then!

The *braque du Bourbonnais* looks, at a distance, uncommonly like the old English bob-tail sheep-dog, but of course he is short-haired. His tail, however, is naturally a regular stump. Query: how did this hereditary short tail occur? In look, this braque *sans queue* is not exactly fascinating. He is a sturdy, stumpy, coarse-looking fellow; but under all this coarseness, this Bourbonnais braque hides an extraordinary intelligence, and most remarkable aptitude. I once sent one over to an old friend, whilst I was in France, about ten years ago, and he wrote back as follows:

"I did not want a sheep-dog! What have you sent me one for?" I replied, "Try him in the field." And he found him such a nice companion, and so well suited to his age (he was nearly seventy), that he declared the dog to be the best he had ever had. This dog had a double nose, a peculiarity which is cried down by some people who have never tried the dogs, but who object, on principle, of course, to anything of which they know absolutely nothing.

Now, in practice, a double-nosed pointer is perhaps not better than an ordinary-nosed one, but he certainly, and emphatically, is not worse, and that is a great thing to say. Moreover, for finding birds in very hot weather (putting aside pace) I have rarely seen anything so good as two or three double-nosed dogs belonging to the breed I am now alluding to, and if prejudices could be put aside, I should like to see some tried by competent authorities, and I warrant these dogs would, judiciously crossed, greatly improve in nose certain breeds of British pointers which have all that could be wished for in pace and style, but are wonderfully deficient in making out their birds, and finding out whether they are still "there," or "have been" there, and are gone.

L'épagneul is not, as his name would imply, a spaniel. An *épagneul* on the Continent is a setter, and the breeds are there simply innumerable, and are not distinguished by any particular names. All *setting* dogs with long and silky hair are called *épagneuls*. Our regular spaniels are called *petits épagneuls* (small spaniels), and are understood to *spring* their game, *not to set* at it. There are but few of the latter class ever used on the Continent, except by Englishmen. Continental sportsmen decidedly have a preference for setting dogs to springers, hence the depreciation in which are held the latter.

The *griffon*, according to my opinion, is simply a cross of rough hound with a smooth pointer or long-haired setter. It is undoubtedly a very ugly dog, coarse, ill-built, but daring, ardent, indefatigable. He will go through a thicket, however impenetrable, and if there is game there out it must come, *nolens volens*; he will find it out, and clear the place of it. The griffon, therefore, has some good qualities, but it is a deuce of a job to break him; and as to classifying him by rights with setting or pointing dogs, why surely there must be somewhere a stretch of imagination. The griffon rarely points at all of his own accord; those who do have been for a long period trained for it, and make a bad sort of point. In short, that sort of dog is not at all bad for beating about a very rough country, but pointing is not by any means their most brilliant point. (Excuse the bad pun.)

And the same is to be said of the *barbet*. The barbet is simply a water-spaniel. Now, my Diver was as good an Irish water-spaniel as ever lived; he certainly used to make a sort of point (a microscopical one), and then up he would get the birds; and so do barbets, only with this difference, that their points are even far less pronounced than my late Diver's short stop. However, barbets are called *chiens d'arrêt* (setting or pointing dogs) on the Continent, and, whilst protesting against the appellation, it is my duty to notice them. They are excellent water dogs, will beat reeds, &c., admirably, find the birds well, bolt them well, and retrieve them capitally; but that is all that can be said in their favour, for there is really no cataleptic aptitude in them, and, therefore, why they should be classed by all French authors as setting dogs fairly beats "this child." In looks, griffons are like coarse setters with something like an otter-hound's coat on. Barbets look, and are, I verily believe, simply poodles. Now, by all that's good, who ever did see a poodle on point—except perhaps on a mutton-chop? No, no, Messrs. Revoil, De la Neuville, and others, as lawyers say, your books on sport are extremely interesting, and very clever, but, may it please your authorships, we can't swallow a pointing or setting poodle, and that is the plain fact.

Should any of my readers wish to get more information on the subject of setting-dogs on the Continent, I would recommend them to procure "La Chasse au Chien d'Arrêt," by the Viscount de la Neuville, and the "Histoire des Chiens," by Revoil. There are, in both works, numerous and somewhat inexcusable mistakes, which the average British sportsman will at once detect, so that he really could not be led away, and the general hints are interesting. To give an instance of the ludicrous errors into which the last-named author was led, the reader will find, page 192 in his book, the following, at any rate, quite new information:

"Cockers and springers are the dogs which Englishmen prefer for *grouse-shooting*, because they never go far from their master, quarter brilliantly, and then *suddenly come to a point!*"

Good, is it not?

CONTINENTAL BOAR-HOUNDS.

I.

BOAR-HOUNDS are not, as their name would seem to imply, used exclusively for boar-hunting—they are employed whenever any powerful and dangerous quarry has to be encountered, whether the said quarry be a boar, a stag, or a wolf; but it must not be thought that these dogs are actually used for "hunting" the quarry. They do nothing of the sort, simply because (notwithstanding their generic name) they are *not* hounds. They could not follow any intricate scent, although I have seen two which could track a fresh scent for some distance. In short, boar-hounds are only slipped when the quarry is in their sight, and their duty is that of fighting it, holding it, and killing it, if they can. When a boar is the object of the chase, the boar-hound's business is to stop him, and hold him tight until the sportsman can fire, or run his spear, or his short hunting-sword, or his boar-bayonet, into the boar's body. In either case, the slightest slackening of the dog's hold would inevitably cause the man's death; hence the saying among foresters, "that a good boar-hound, once he has got hold of the swine's ears, must never let go but when the swine is dead." This little job of seizing the boar's ears is wonderfully ticklish, for close to the swine's ears are his tusks, and these are most deadly instruments of warfare, and he knows it. To give an idea of the irresistible power of these tusks, I may state that I have seen two or three boars sharpening them on oak-trees, and a steel chisel could hardly have made a more decided indentation. I have also, unfortunately, seen dogs killed outright, and not a few maimed, by charges of wild-boars.

Now it will readily be admitted that an animal who can indent oak-wood, kill a powerful dog at a single upward switch of his snout, and will charge through anything, is not exactly a pleasant customer to deal with when roused. It is a treat to see him bristle when he spies the dogs; his grunts are simply awful; and anything more expressive of fury and rage than his general countenance and ways cannot be imagined. It is therefore a most dangerous undertaking to go and tackle him in that state; yet this is exactly what boar-hounds are called upon to do. It takes, therefore, a vast amount of pluck, and a good deal of substance and power withal, to enter the field against such odds, but these properties and qualities are pre-eminently shown in the average boar-hound. Several have been exhibited at our shows, and a good idea may be formed of their style, at any rate, by studying the best specimens (very fair ones indeed) among those that have appeared.

A young boar-hound is entered only when full-grown, and even then he is slipped, for the first time, at a full-grown boar only when an experienced dog has already taken hold, so that he should not encounter too heavy odds on his first trial. It is very rare that the young dog requires any further tuition, but he must be taught never to let go (when once he has seized hold), until the boar is dead. This is easily taught to the puppies by making them seize a towel, and encouraging them to resist all attempts to take it away from them. I have seen some that positively would not surrender it on any terms for hours, and have witnessed one hoisted up to a loft-window by his keeper times out of number. When exhibitions of fighting animals were not only legal but encouraged, it was a very common sight to see a dog trained to that sort of thing, being, before the paying public, hoisted many yards in the air by making him seize a towel tied to a long rope, which ran over a pulley fixed at the top of the building; and I have now before me an original bill of the entertainment provided for the lovers of that sort of thing and of fighting animals, an extract from which will be given in the course of these papers.

Now the modern boar-hound exhibits the same tenacity of hold, especially when pitted against an animal. It is not uncommon for one dog to hold hard on a strong boar until the other dogs can seize hold too, and the contest is generally of the fiercest description. When slipped at a boar or at a stag, the boar-hounds run with their ordinary collars on, and sometimes with none, but the attendants have all that is necessary to secure them, and couple or leash them afterwards, when the affair is over. When, however, a wolf is the quarry in view, the boar-hounds invariably wear spiked collars as a protection for their necks against the almost irresistible bites of the wolf. For the same reason all boar-hounds likely to have to deal with wolves have their ears cropped as short as possible. In short, these dogs are got up quite in fighting trim, so as to offer no easily-got-at hold to the wolves.

No boar-hound who sees active service can escape being scarred at some period or other of his career. The slightest slip or mistake in making his rush is sure to give the wild boar a chance to score of which he is never slow to avail himself, and some of the dogs are literally disembowelled. It is astonishing how quickly these wounded dogs do recover when no vital part has actually been reached. I have now in my mind's eye an old boar-hound who works with a forester in Bohemia, and the old dog has had his belly ripped open and sewn up again five or six times. He has had, besides, many very ugly gashes over the neck and chest; but he goes as well as ever (or rather used to when I was there), though he ran rather stiff when first started. This soon wore off, however, and he was certainly a very accomplished boar-holder then.

Generally speaking, a couple of good boar-hounds are a match for any wolf—*i.e.* they are sure to kill it between them. There are, however, boar-hounds who single-handed can master a wolf; but these are few and far between, because the power of jaw of the wolf and the extraordinary length of his "holders" are far superior to that of any ordinary dog, even of large size. If, therefore, only one boar-hound be pitted against a full-grown wolf the chances are greatly in favour of the wild animal; but if two boar-hounds be at it, then they will make short work of him, especially if they are well cropped and are wearing their spiked collars. The latter bother a wolf awfully, and well it might, for it deprives him of his natural hold.

The thorough training of boar-hounds is necessarily a matter of time and practice. An experienced boar-hound seizes a wolf or a stag by the throat; but he makes no such mistake with a wild-boar. The dogs never stand directly in front of the boar, whereas the tactics of the boar are always to keep the dogs in front of his tusks if he can. Therefore, the boar-hounds must resort to a little manœuvre; they must avoid the boar's rushes, turn him, then run alongside of him, seize his ears firmly, and hang back with all their might, and hold tight in spite of all his shakings, rushes, and attempts to bolt. That this last part of the programme is no joke will be readily admitted, and it often happens that such is the strength and irresistible power of the beast that he will drag along for hundreds of yards a set of powerful dogs which half-a-dozen men could hardly hold back. One can always mark in the forests the very spot where the boar-hounds took hold, by the marks of their paws alongside the boar's track. It looks as though the mossy ground had been ploughed along all the way up to where the boar came to a standstill, and received his *coup de grâce*. Sometimes it will happen that one of the dogs gets a "poor" hold, or that the boar's ears, having been previously torn in some encounter, one of the dogs misses a sound piece, in which case the boar gets rid of that dog, and turns at once to face the other, and woe betide him if he does not keep his eyes well skinned! In this case the discomfited hounds generally seize the boar's hind legs; but they cannot kill a full-grown boar, the sportsman must come forward to do it, and it is an extremely dangerous sort of business. I am not a greater coward than other people, I believe; but I never could see the fun of going on foot, with a short sword, to stab an animal which, infuriated by pain, would indubitably send you into the next world should one of the dogs just then relax his hold. I have killed perhaps a score of wild-boars on the Continent, and to some of them I have been a great deal nearer than I liked; but I think people will look upon it as a sign of soundness of my head when I state that I never walked up to their snouts, but invariably despatched them with a gun or with a rifle. True, in some of these cases, I might have hit one of the dogs, but then I did not; and if I had, why I would rather have accidentally killed a dog than run the risk of being myself killed, or at least maimed for life. Some continental sportsmen, however, take a sort of pride in doing foolhardy tricks. As long as they are successful, these tricks only make beholders tremble for the safety of the venturesome fellows; but when some day they miss their stroke, and an accident takes place, all said and done, people cannot help exclaiming, " Serve them right, for what business had they to run such risks?"

Boar-hounds, however, are gradually getting into disuse, simply because killing wild-boars nowadays is getting more and more a matter of hunting, and less and less a matter of shooting. Wherever wild-boars are known to turn up, packs of hounds are invariably got up now, so as to give the sportsmen as much fun out of each individual boar as possible. So much so that positively even if the boar gives a chance of being shot, at the very beginning of the hunt, the sportsmen refrain from taking advantage of the opportunity, so as to have the pleasure of hunting the beast at least some hours before despatching it. This being so, boar-hounds would be there out of place. Ordinary hounds do the business of driving the boar, as long as he chooses to be driven. When he (the boar) gets tired of it, he stops and faces the pack, and, as a matter of fact, would very quickly dispose of the whole lot unless the sportsmen turn up and kill him. No ordinary hound has the shadow of a chance with a boar. It is not unusual for half a pack to be killed or maimed, and the rest put *en déroute* by a single old boar. The reason why is simply a want of sufficient weight and strength on the part of ordinary hounds. In short, none but the most powerful dogs can at all hold their own with boars. These powerful dogs must also be very nimble, be in good wind, and be endowed with unflinching pluck. A good boar-hound must be an enormous animal, moving, nevertheless, with as much comparative ease as a working fox-terrier; he must have powerful loins, a stout neck, a broad bull-terrier face on a large scale, iron jaws, good thighs and legs; he must run true (no waddling about, as one will notice in eight mastiffs out of a dozen); he must have excellent "holders," and his temper must be "shady." With these qualifications and due practice, the dog will be bound to turn out A 1. The markings and coats of boar-hounds are by foresters indifferently looked upon. I have seen rough-coated dogs with red-and-white patches; I have seen also smooth blacks and blues and brindles, and also black-and-whites and brindle-and-whites; in short, there is no special "tint" yet for boar-hounds. Should they, however, become regular "show-fancy," no doubt this or that colour will be prohibited, and probably a snip of white on one toe or on the face will eventually disqualify an otherwise eligible member from taking any prize.

CONTINENTAL BOAR-HOUNDS.

II.

For actual use there are yet a few boar-hounds bred and trained, but, as I have shown, the great value now attached to the sport of hunting is slowly, but safely, driving the boar-hound from his legitimate employment. Eventually he will be an extinct race, at least for boar-killing; but as long as the law in the Low Countries will allow dogs to be used as beasts of draught, probably a good many will still be reared, at least for that purpose. In Belgium, on any market-day, at any town in the Low Countries, hundreds of these dogs may be seen in harness; and I may add that I am surprised that some of these have not been secured by English exhibitors for show purposes. I remember one which was a marvellously well-shaped monster. He was the size of a donkey nearly, and certainly the sturdiest and biggest dog of any breed I have seen, and I have seen a few.

As regards the use of boar-hounds for drawing carts, I am quite at variance with those who patronise that sort of thing. The poor animals are cowed and shamefully overworked. It is not uncommon on a lonely road to meet three or four men piled up on a tiny cart, in the shafts of which one or two poor dogs, with their tongues out, are labouring painfully to keep "on the trot." I think that if a man cannot afford a proper beast of draught he ought to do the pulling himself. Dogs are not intended by nature to be put to such work. True, in northern regions they are so used, but then no other motive power is available there, and that makes all the difference. As concerns the continent of Europe, there is no such dire necessity, and therefore the whole system ought to be abolished. I remember reading somewhere that harness-dogs in Belgium were very happy and good-tempered. Such is not the fact, and the best proof is that by law the owners of such dogs are obliged to secure them, when taken off the shafts, in such a manner that they should be unable to come at anybody or anything. As a matter of fact, even when in harness, these dogs always try to reach one another, and I have frequently observed two or three carts racing, the dogs trying to seize each other, and this in spite of all the efforts of their drivers, who eventually had to dismount in order to prevent a "battle royal."

By-the-way, although pitched battles are forbidden by law, many such events still take place for small wagers. Many of the continental dog-owners are proud of their dogs' capabilities in that line, and are always ready to pit them against all-comers. If caught, many excuses can readily be put forward. "It could not be helped; the dogs broke loose and assailed each other, and they could not be separated until they had had their fling," &c. That the majority of boar-hounds are *primâ facie* always willing to join in anything of the sort is tolerably well known. In former times they were the chief combatants in the arenas in France, Belgium, Alsace, and Bavaria. I have shot wolves and boars in Alsace with two boar-hounds that had repeatedly fought bears, wolves, and hyenas, in public, in years happily gone by. They in private fought a bear during my stay in the province, but I did not see the affair, having declined to countenance the proceedings. That sort of thing, however, is gradually dying out, but that it exists still, anyone may readily convince himself by going into a foresters' village with a dog or any other animal, and offering covertly to back him against the foresters' boar-hounds. A match, or several matches, will very soon be made, on the strict Q.T. of course. In former times, however, such things were done openly and legally. Bands were engaged, and the military kept the way open for intending visitors, such was the crush of spectators.

I have now before me the "bill of fare" of such an exhibition, and beg to give a translation thereof *in extenso*, as a curiosity in connection with my subject, for, be it known that, with the exception of a few smaller dogs used for baiting, all the more violent onslaughts and all the killing business were performed by boar-hounds. The following is taken from *The Mirror*, 1829, who copied it from the original:

"BARRIÈRE DU COMBAT, ANCIEN CHEMIN DE PANTIN, PARIS.

" The Sieur Gerot, successor to the Sieur Mouroy, proprietor of the establishment hitherto known under the denomination of the *Combat des Animaux*, has the honour of informing the public that his exercises will take place *every Sunday* and holiday.—To please the public, he will promise little, keep more than what is promised, and thus surprise agreeably.

"To-morrow, Sunday, the 8th of May, 1825, will be a grand combat of a young and vigorous bull. This furious animal, without equal for agility and ferocity, will be attacked vigorously by dogs of the greatest force and first-rate shape, who will relieve one another turn about. Messieurs the amateurs, and also the *bourgeois*, will have the liberty of letting loose their dogs against the indomitable animal.

"The bear of Poland, lately arrived at the menagerie of the *Combat du Taureau*, and who has never appeared or fought in the arena. This young and vigorous animal will fight for the first time.

"The famous wild-boar of the Black Forest will be hunted, and pursued by dogs trained to this kind of exercise.

"The wolf of the forest of Ardennes will fight, and be hunted and pursued in an astonishing manner.

"The combat will be concluded by the raising of the famous bulldog" (in the original *bouldogue*) "'Maroquin,' so well known for the force of his jaw, to more than fifty feet high, in a brilliant firework of a new and very extraordinary nature.

"*Les fanfares*, sporting airs suitable to this kind of amusement, will be performed turn about.

"Price of admission—Pit, 75c. (7½d.) ; Amphitheatre, 1f.; Boxes, 2f. The office will be opened at two o'clock, and the diversions will commence at five. In case of bad weather the whole place is covered. Bear's grease is sold for the cure of rheumatic pains, freckles, and other complaints. Sieur Gerot sells and buys all sorts of dogs for the protection of country and town houses, cures them of sickness and wounds, and takes them to keep. Tickets once taken, the money will not be returned. Children under seven years of age will only pay half-price. A great battle every Monday."

In another of these bills was the following assurance, which must have been highly satisfactory to messieurs the amateurs: "Nothing shall be neglected to render the combats obstinate."

In Boulogne and other towns besides Paris, such entertainments were always a sure "draw." A contributor to *The Mirror* of the same date says that he saw "on the Saturday before one of these 'combats,' a bill of fare stuck upon the wall, in which was a list of *at least forty* poor beasts who were condemned to be tortured for the *amusement* of the public." In this bill there were a *wolf and a donkey* which were to be the principal combatants, though to be sure there were numerous *horses* and *dogs*, which were paired, bears and wolves, &c. &c., in great numbers. The prices were fixed at *un franc aux premières*, and *dix sous aux secondes*.

At one o'clock the crowd was so great that the military (as usual) were brought out to keep back those "whose spirits were willing, but whose *pockets* were *light*," from having a sight, and those people *actually* stood there *five hours*—*i.e.* till the baiting was over, to *hear* what they could, as there was a full military band playing all the while to *inspire* the combatants."

Erkmann-Chatrian describe at full length such a performance in their celebrated novel, "Le Combat d'Ours." In that description I learnt, to my infinite astonishment, that donkeys were excellent fighters. I forget now how *the* donkey of the performance fared, and not having the work at hand to refer to, I am unable to refresh my memory; but, as far as I can recollect, he made a most determined resistance, disabling all the dogs.

It cannot be denied that such exhibitions were very debasing. In the open forests, where wolf or boar have, with the boar-hound, pretty equal chances of success, such contests are fair, being necessary; but the idea of keeping animals in confinement, to be turned loose in an enclosed arena, and there to be assailed by ferocious dogs, is simply revolting. That such things should "draw," however, is not to be wondered at. The novelty of the thing, and the morbid curiosity of the masses, are quite sufficient to account for the crowds which usually flock to see these "exercises," as the managers, curiously enough, called these exhibitions. The boar-hound of to-day is just as ready as his ancestors to enter into such contests. I have seen a score of working boar-hounds which could be slipped at any living animal by their masters, and who would take their death rather than cave in. Good specimens of the breed are to be found in Germany, Denmark, Holland, Belgium, Bavaria, Alsace, and France. They are, generically, called Danish boar-hounds, but whether they really originated from Denmark or not I am unable to say. According to the specimens I have seen, the Danish (proper) boar-hounds have somewhat longer and sharper muzzles than the Alsatian or French or Belgian bred dogs; but of course there is no deciding on such a question by judging from a score of dogs or so only. As watch-dogs, boar-hounds are unrivalled. They never sleep at night, but roam about over the premises; and woe betide the evil-doer upon whom they may come! They are also frequently used as night-dogs by keepers, and owing to their great strength and weight they easily overpower any man, although muzzled when slipped.

In some places on the Continent it is not unusual to see some of these dogs loose in the villages, but they almost invariably wear then a thick piece of wood hanging from their collar between their forelegs, so as to prevent them from fighting among themselves, and to trip them up if they should attempt to run after something or somebody. In short, preventive measures must necessarily be taken wherever such powerful customers are employed, for otherwise accidents would certainly happen far more frequently than they do now.

At any rate, for his master, a boar-hound is the very embodiment of what a dog should be. He will protect both him or his property to the last drop of his blood; he will take punishment unflinchingly; he is ever on the alert; and at the first sign of danger he is "all there," and courts the battle. Such is the character of the boar-hounds I have seen.

BOAR AND WOLF-HUNTING.

IN my former chapters I treated of the wolf-hounds used *officially* by the equipages of *louveterie*, and I have also considered the boar-hounds as used privately by foresters for *seizing* the boar or *killing* the wolf. I am now going to enter into a description of the *packs* of hounds used on the Continent, by private sportsmen, for both wolf and boar *hunting*.

There are some large packs (especially in Germany and in France) used almost exclusively for hunting both animals. By almost exclusively I mean that the gun and the hunting-knife are with these packs resorted to only when the hunted animal is brought to bay: in contradistinction with the practice of those men who try to clip either brute as soon as ever they get the chance, with or without a run.

In either case the preliminary proceedings are exactly similar—in this wise, that one of the whips goes beforehand (either late the previous evening or very early in the morning) to reconnoitre with a lymer the whereabouts of the quarry. This is very delicate work. A wild-boar or a wolf are on a perpetual look-out; I verily believe that they sleep with at least *one* eye open, and *both* ears always on the alert. The slightest unusual noise startles them, and they both will make off if they are at all suspicious that everything is not altogether aboveboard around them. They skedaddle however in two different ways; the wolf sneaks quietly along, stretching himself well, but picking out his ground, so as to make no noise by running on pebbles, stones, or rocks; he even takes care not to brush a bush violently; in short, he positively vanishes without any outward warning being given of his egress, and were it not that the hounds can make out easily his strong scent, and let you know it at once when crossing his track, a sportsman might be within a few yards of a runaway wolf, and not be aware of it.

A wild-boar acts totally different. Whether he be in his lair, or feeding, or wallowing in a pond, the moment something unusual gives him a hint that it will be better for him to be "scarce," he erects his head, winds the breeze, flaps his ears, and grunts, almost inaudibly at first; but, should the alarm prove correct, he gives vent to his feelings in a terrified grunt as loud as a horse's neigh, and forthwith he bolts straight away through anything, thicket, bushes, or open; off he goes like an arrow, piercing his way through the thickest of underwoods with the greatest of ease and clattering along over rocky ground with a total disregard of the probability that someone will hear him. Thus anyone who is posted around a wood where a wild boar is being roused by the hounds, always gets a timely warning of the boar's approach by the extraordinary clatter he kicks up along his headlong course; whereas for a wolf the sportsman must simply trust to his eyesight to detect him when he breaks, because he comes along quite silently, like a cat. But whatever difference there may be in the style of the wolf and boar when they are bolting, there is a great similarity in the readiness with which they take the alarm, and in the quickness of perception with which they detect the approach of any enemy.

This being so, the *piqueur* (whip), whose duty it is to *faire le bois* (literally, "make the wood;" *i.e.* to ascertain the whereabouts of the quarry in the covert), must proceed with the greatest caution, so as not to alarm the animal. Hence the great demand on the Continent for men who are well versed in woodcraft to act as *piqueurs*, either to a nobleman's large pack or for a private sportsman's two or three couples.

The way in which these *piqueurs* proceed is very simple, but it requires considerable experience to know when to go on and when to stop, and they must be able to tell at a glance what are the various footprints left in the soft banks, whether they are old or fresh marks; whether the animal was going along quietly and undisturbed, or whether, on the contrary, he was at speed and going extended; and, in the latter case, whether he was only frightened or absolutely pursued; and if so, what was on his track—men, hounds, or curs, or boarhounds. Some of these men, moreover, will tell at a glance the sex, size, and probable age of the animal by his slots and marks, and this knowledge, it need not be remarked, is *not* "acquired in twelve lessons (ahem!) like perfect penmanship;" but there are some infallible rules of the craft which are, nevertheless, easily acquired, and so far as they go they are very handy.

Thus if the sportsman has a wood near a village whose inhabitants keep pigs, and allow them (as is frequently the case on the Continent) to forage for themselves about the covert, it may happen that the said pigs will wander a considerable way from the village, and give the sportsman a false alert by their footmarks in a distant part of the covert where he could only expect wild-boars to turn up. But if the sportsman bears in mind that boars when undisturbed invariably place their hind feet in the marks left by their fore-feet, whereas pigs tread with four distinct marks, he can put his mind at rest at once by a summary inspection of the footprints. I have been on sundry occasions much amused by a certain German *piqueur's* remarks. This fellow would tell by their marks actually whose pigs had been about. He knew every individual pig's "stamps" as he used to call them. "There went," he would say, "old Mother Keppell's old sow; you can see, sir, how wide she treads, as compared with the blacksmith's old boar!"

As for wolves, the two distinctive marks whereby the eye can detect their surreptitious presence are, *firstly*, their footprints, which show a large "ball" and elongated toes, thereby differing from a large dog's footprints, inasmuch as the dog's toes tread wide of each other, whereas the wolf treads in rabbit or hare fashion, his toes being all pointed forward; *secondly*, the wolf's excrements are unmistakable, and cannot possibly be taken for a dog's. Of course the *piqueur*, when "doing the wood," takes note of all he sees, and supposing he comes on several marks of different animals, he compares them all, and chooses always the largest and oldest animal's track as the one he will follow. If the covert is very extensive he puts his lymer at once on the scent, and holding him tight, they both creep along in perfect silence, the "gloating" of the hound alone testifying to his being on the right track. This lymer never "opens." He is absolutely mute when thus engaged. Several breeds are used as lymers; one of the best is that in which a wolf-cross is to be traced, because the lymer takes readily from his ancestor's blood the habit of going and hunting in silence, and he also inherits a most acute sense of smell. The power of scent of some of these lymers is positively extraordinary. Hours after the quarry has passed they yet can unravel its track unerringly. There are some lymers which although when tracking run perfectly mute, yet when running with the rest of the pack give tongue, but they never give it so soundly and so persistently as the ordinary hounds. Their tracking, training, and probably also their special breeding, always keep them a great deal less noisy than the other hounds.

When actually tracking a boar or a wolf, it is always easy to tell whether a scent be warm or cold from the lymer's behaviour; and the *piqueur*, when thus engaged, must note carefully how the lymer behaves, so as not to go too near the animal whose whereabouts he wants to ascertain. Thus, as long as the lymer "feathers along," all is well, but the moment he pulls very hard on the leash, and begins "gloating" noisily, the whip must stop him and retrace his footsteps. Then he must go round for the next ride, or round the covert if it is a small one, and put the lymer on again to hunt for the scent. If the lymer picks it up and follows it, the quarry is still farther away, and must be sought for again in the next bit of covert in the same manner. But if the lymer finds nothing in the ride or on the outskirts, and the *piqueur* can detect no "marks," then he goes home, perfectly satisfied that the quarry is in the covert, and he will bring his hounds on it with certainty in the morning. In extensive coverts it is usual for the *piqueurs* to mark the place where the quarry has entered the wood by breaking several branches of the trees right and left of the track, and sometimes sticking them in the ground, or else allowing them to hang half broken from the trees as a sort of landmark for himself or the huntsman on the morrow. This is called, technically, in *vénerie, faire la brisée*, literally, " to make the breakage "—*i.e.* break branches to mark the place where the beast actually entered the covert.

From this style of doing things, it will be seen that the two most important points in connection with a pack of boar or wolf-hounds are, first, an experienced *piqueur*; and, secondly, one or two, or more good lymers. Without these no sport is possible; for if the beasts be not, so to speak, "spotted" over-night, it is a perfect "toss-up" whether they will be found on the following day.

In cases of emergency, such as when it is likely that the boar or the wolf will escape if hunted in the usual manner, or when time presses, some men kill it by tracking it outright to its lair, and shooting it there. In this case, for a boar, the lymer alone is used, and he is kept on the leash until the beast's stronghold is reached, when, if the boar is invisible, the lymer is slipped in order to arouse him, and bring him out in front of the guns; but if the boar can be at all seen without slipping the lymer, it is fired at there and then without further delay. I have described such an expedition, undertaken by myself and a keeper, in Vol, I.

When a wolf is the quarry the lymer is never slipped at all at him alone, because it would be certain death to the hound. With a boar it is different—the boar charges straight and stiff, and cannot turn readily in his charge; so the lymer can always, if pretty nimble, and used to that sort of affair, escape its rushes; but a wolf is a different customer altogether. He is quick and sharp, and bites with a strength, a ferocity, and a pertinacity, which are simply irresistible. No living hound could, alone, withstand a full-grown wolf's onslaught.

The breeds of boar or wolf-lymers vary exceedingly. I have seen about a dozen lymers. One was the offspring of a Spanish pointer-dog with a fox-hound bitch; another was, in looks, a regular pointer; another was a distant wolf-cross with hound blood; and the others were indubitably hounds of sundry French and German breeds, which, through sheer training and practice, tracked mute when held in hand. It stands to reason that if a young hound which is leashed, and being thus at all times at the discretion of his trainer, is punished whenever it opens, it will undoubtedly take to hunting mute, at least as long as the trainer's hand is nigh; but there is no doubt that the best of the lymers I saw was the one whose cross was wolf in some degree, and the next best the pointer-and-hound cross. The others "gloated" too loud for near work in tracking, and they needed constant attention and supervision when thus engaged.

Concerning the packs, a couple of hounds well entered will drive either boar or wolf comfortably, but they must be backed by the gun, or else they must eschew anything like a battle. As regards actual hunting, a couple is as good as forty couples, barring the music of course. Now some men like the melody of a large pack. I do; I think nothing is more stirring. But of course tastes differ, and means must also be consulted; hence the man who cannot afford to buy and to keep a large pack must perforce be satisfied with a couple or two, and must do his best with them. With even that small number of hounds, if they know what they are about, a good deal can be done in the way of boar and wolf-hunting and shooting. There are some foresters who clip two or three scores every season, besides many deer and roebuck, with sometimes only one hound; but then these men know every point of vantage, and are crack shooters, who very rarely miss their mark.

All sorts of hounds are to be seen on the Continent used for boar and wolf-hunting by private individuals, from the tiny French *bassets à jambes torses* and the German dachshunds, up to the monstrous Artois, Vendée, and Poitou hounds, rough and smooth, and their other innumerable varieties, any hound that *will* follow the scent is enlisted in the fray; and it all depends, from the nature of the covert and from the means of the sportsman, what hounds and how many he will use for the sport. Whatever, however, these hounds may be, and whether the sportsman hunts alone with a hound or two, or he hunts in company, and with a large pack, the quarry is always, whenever possible, first tracked with a lymer beforehand, and the hounds are slipped in the morning at the *brisée*. It is only now and then, and by rare chance, that hounds come, by great luck, upon either a wolf or a boar, because the presence of either in a district being almost always known as soon as they turn up, the sportsmen then invariably resort to the scientific rules of *vênerie*, in order to make the most of their sport.

THE WORKING OF SPORTING DOGS

AT FIELD TRIALS AND IN THE FIELD.

I.

THERE can be no doubt in the minds of all who are interested in the subject that a certain amount of artificiality has been gradually creeping into the working of pointers and setters at field trials—*i.e.* many of the dogs are being trained especially for field trials, and run therein in a manner which would not be quite admitted for *bonâ-fide* private sport; and I will show it.

In two points is this artificiality particularly striking, viz., in quartering and in backing.

It cannot be denied that pace is a charming accomplishment; and, therefore, I would not by any means advise slower ranging, provided there be "nose" to go with "legs"—ay, there's the rub. Many dogs go "full tilt," like blind moles, and have no more nose than a watering-can. In such cases pace is evidently a mistake. But that is not the point about which I just now wish to argue. I want to point out that, with a laudable desire to secure quickly more points than their rivals, but with a mistaken notion as to the best way of securing these points, the dogs are taught to start at full-speed straight down their fields; and it is self-evident that such running cannot be called good quartering, since by both dogs the left and right corners of each field are left perfectly untouched; and all those sportsmen who have attended field trials know that almost invariably, when a brace of dogs have done with a field and the crowd cross that field to reach a fresh one, the said crowd almost invariably walk up birds. Now this, I say, ought not to be. If we were actually shooting, should we allow such a state of affairs? Certainly not. *Ergo*, the quartering at field trials is highly deficient; and my statement that the ranging is artificial is correct.

But why should it be so? Is it not a patent mistake to all thinking men. Since the crowd flush birds where the dogs ought to have gone, but have not been, and never (or rarely) do go systematically, is it not perfectly clear that the dog who would be taught to quarter as though for the gun would have more chance to score quickly than his rivals, since almost in his first stride about his own side he could find birds? I can give a striking instance to the point. The Duke of Westminster's little black-and-white pointer dog, Rector, who won at Shrewsbury in the All-aged Stakes or County Stakes (I forget which now), two years ago, won simply because he really *did* quarter well his fields. I do not mean to set him up, though, as a star of extraordinary magnitude; he is a slower ranger than most of his competitors, and I do not admire slow work; but *his* slower work did beat *their* pace, and his victory was attributable simply to his very careful quartering of every bit of ground. Brailsford, who broke and worked him, told me that the dog was A1 for private sport, and

I fully believe him, as he is just the sort of dog that won't mind investigating the most likely spots, *i.e.* the corners at which the fast-ranging, devil-may-care, usual run of field trialers turn up their noses. The fact is, they are not taught to do it; but that ought to be condemned. Let the dogs beat their fields properly; let the judges reward, by points, those who quarter well their ground, and let them penalise all dogs who leave birds behind them; that is the way to do it, and I warrant we should find soon a marked improvement in, at any rate, the ranging. As matters now stand, most field-trial dogs are far from perfect for private sport, and I have pointed out one of their most glaring defects. It is not pleasant when a man buys such a dog, with a high reputation, to find that, like a weedy racehorse, fit only for racing purposes, the dog is only good for public exhibition, and cannot be put to any useful work. I now come to the very deficient backing which I have frequently observed.

Would anyone be surprised to hear that pointers and setters learn (precious quickly, too) to work "cunning?" Well, they do, and do it remarkably well, too; but we cannot blame the dogs. It is quite natural that the spirit of emulation should induce them to do so. Their breakers, however, ought to see to it, and should check that sort of thing in the bud. I am afraid, however, the reverse is the case. The race for honours is so severe that one is apt to take every advantage. Now "all is fair in love and in war," we are told, but "all" ought not to be fair at field trials, and I think something ought to be done to prevent anything which is not strictly correct and *de bon ton* in such a grand sport.

Of course, by working "cunning," I do not mean that

the pointers or setters run like cunning greyhounds—*i.e.* bide their time. No, they would "cut their throats" by so doing; for in field trials, he who is first has the best chance to "find." What I mean is that when a dog, being on point, his adversary, when he sees him, instead of at once backing him, turns away on another sweep purposely, so as to find birds himself rather than back the other dog, then I say this sort of thing is not admissible, and it ought to penalise the dog whenever practised.

I could give several instances of otherwise very good dogs who have fallen into this evil habit; and I could give glaring instances in which the attention of the judges was called to the fact, and, *mirabile dictu*, they declined to notice it, and turned a deaf ear to "the charmer's entreaties." I have no wish to give the dogs' names. I am on friendly terms with most field-trial sportsmen, and naturally wish to remain so as far as possible; and I know, feelingly, that finding fault with a man's own dog is next door to calling the man names. "A nod is as good as a wink to a blind horse." Those field-trial goers who will read this will know I am right, and will say: "Ay, such a dog acted thus in such-and-such stakes," and so forth; *ergo*, here is another bit of artificiality with which we can very well dispense. In fact, if anything, it is worse than deficient ranging or quartering, and I certainly opine that a dog that wilfully refuses to back ought to be put out, or at any rate be severely penalised, because this wilfulness arises simply from the breaker's fault—he encourages his dog in it.

For instance. Two dogs are slipped, A and B. A falls on point; B, coming up, sees A, but instead of dropping, as some do, or simply backing, he turns away, deliberately ranges again, and soon he also gets a point.

Well, I say that B is working "cunning." He has failed to back, which is bad; he has gone away deliberately, which is worse still; and his stolen "point" is nothing more nor less than a barefaced robbery. But what do we see? Why, some judges, when A gets on his "point," take note of it, mentally or otherwise; but when B comes along and turns back, they say: "Oh! he did not see A on point, I suppose; and now, lo! he has a point too. Well done B!" Well, that may be all right in their estimation; but I humbly think it is all wrong. If there is no accident of ground between the dogs, B must have seen A. Nay, I have seen specimens of the B style deliberately look at A for two or three seconds, and turn back with malice prepense. In private work I have seen many dogs do that sort of thing, too, wilfully. In private, however, it might be of little consequence; but at public trials such a thing is of vital importance, and the dog who wilfully declines to back, at once and without hesitation, and, on the contrary, starts back on his own account, I have no hesitation in saying is but an imperfectly broken dog, and therefore ought to be penalised, more or less heavily, or even put out as unbroken. And when B's breaker, instead of standing still when A is on point, walks away towards his dog, he virtually encourages his dog to work "cunning." Some breakers in such cases have always the stereotyped excuses ready: "My dog was feathering; he was on scent; some birds were there," &c. This is all very well, and it may be but the strict truth now and then; but no matter whether it be so or not, the moment one of the dogs is on point both breakers ought to stop, and stand perfectly still.

If their dogs are well broken, they will do their work well without the men's help. If the dogs require signs, calls, shouts, or whistling to, they are not perfect. (Of course, I mean this for public trials, when perfection, or next door to it, alone is to be considered.) And by-the-way it is really astonishing to find how much time is wasted at field trials over dogs that have not the remotest chance of winning. Why should a dog's trial be protracted, if the dog has worked so indifferently, or misbehaved himself in such a manner as to render his chances of winning totally nil? It may be that the judges wish to please the owner by giving him, at any rate, a "run for his money;" but such considerations ought to have no weight in public performances. For instance, when a dog only drops when ordered to, and persists in disregarding wing, or gun, or fur, he ought to be put out there and then. Thus half the time at least would be saved which is now simply wasted. Concerning the actual working of the dogs, silence ought to be as strictly the rule as possible; and I confess I do not like to hear an otherwise very clever breaker call out "Whoâ!" in a stentorian voice whenever his dogs get on point. Perhaps he does it in order to call the judges' attention to that fact; but if so, it is a plan which is truly to be deprecated. Holding up his hand would answer quite as well. Were every breaker to call out "whoâ!" whenever points are being got upon, there is no reason why they should not shout "drop!" for dropping; "back!" for backing, &c.; and then, what with shouting and whistling, &c., field trials would become a sort of bear-garden. If, on the other hand, only one man uses his voice, he by so doing bothers the other man's dog, who does not know what is meant, and is puzzled how to act.

I am aware that a good deal of warmth and feeling has been creeping into the sport, but it must not be allowed to spoil it notwithstanding; and I trust that such remarks as I am making will be taken in as fair a spirit as they are given; failing which, why, I will run the risk of displeasing a very few in order to agree with the many.

Respecting the different ways in which the various dogs take their points, opinions differ. Some dogs drop at once, and are thus really dropped to the subsequent wing, fur, or gun. So far so good; but I, and many others, like to see a dog standing his birds or fur well. It is a superb position, and when he drops, as though shot, to wing, hare, or gun, the performance is all the more meritorious, on both the dog and the breaker's part.

Then, again, some dogs when once they have dropped (either to hand or game or gun) have to be walked to by their keeper before starting again on their ranging. I think that such a system is a mistake, involving as it does some very unnecessary hard work on the part of the breaker or of the sportsman who works the dogs. How would a shooter, when working a brace of pointers or setters, like the tedious bother of having to walk to each of his dogs each time they had dropped? Why such an artificial and very tiring process? Why not train the dogs to go on again, at a wave of the hand for instance? Some breakers prefer this walking up to their dogs, because their near presence steadies their dogs, as a matter of course; but again I repeat that at field trials there ought to be no necessity for "steadying," and so forth—in short, none but absolutely perfect dogs ought to be seen there, and they ought to be worked there as they would be worked by a private sportsman in search of sport over his manor, *i.e.*

there ought to be no special training required for field-trial performances. The best dogs, then, ought to be also the best everyday workers; and thus, by doing away with all artificiality, we should come to such a degree of practical excellence in our setting-dogs that the general public would come to look upon investing in them with a degree of confidence which they do not now feel. Many private sportsmen look upon a field-trial dog as a luxury of the racehorse kind, *i.e.* fit for no earthly use beyond his original sphere, *i.e.* field-trial running. That such is not the case, however, now with many field-trial dogs is patent to all who attend field trials; but that it is but too true of a great many more is also very evident. In short, dogs ought not to be kept and broken exclusively for field trials, if the public at large are expected to take an interest therein; and when one hears practical sportsmen, after due consideration, declare that public trials are wrongly carried out, depend upon it "there is something rotten in the state of Denmark."

I wanted to point out one or two more unsatisfactory features of the sport, but, finding that this chapter has grown to such a length, I must reluctantly pull up, and put off further remarks for the next.

THE WORKING OF SPORTING DOGS

AT FIELD TRIALS AND IN THE FIELD.

II.

THE only objection which I have heard against my views on the above subject, as expressed in my last chapter, which originally appeared in *The Field*, is the following. Although in private there is no occasion for the sportsman (or breaker) to train the dogs to remain dropped until he has walked up to them, it is urged that in public work, such as at field trials, it is desirable to do so, because the dogs, seeing so many people about them, are apt to run wild, and therefore the now and then near presence of their breaker or master is decidedly apt to make them recollect themselves—*i.e.* steady them.

There is sound reason in this objection, but there are no insuperable difficulties in the way of removing it; and it might easily be arranged to occasionally run the dogs, when broken, in the presence of some score of strangers, just to get them used to the eventual sight of a crowd. Besides this, on the whole, I have a fancy that it is only young and high-spirited dogs that would be so much influenced as to get the standard of their work lowered. Old "stagers" do not care a rush whether two men or fifty men are looking on, and if at all flushed, it is more by the sight of other dogs actually running, than by anything else. Thus you will see sometimes a breaker with two or three leashed dogs, looking on a brace actually running under the very noses of his charges. What are the consequences? Why, the leashed dogs, naturally enough, struggle to their utmost to get loose and have themselves a spin. It is not pleasant to have to look on whilst others are enjoying themselves, they presumably think; and hence, being detained by force, and yet tantalised by the sight of their *confrères* at work, they literally work themselves into a frenzy, and no wonder that, when their turn to run happens to come, they at first rush about wildly and blindly. Yet the majority of the breakers do not seem to be aware of the injurious effects of this contemplation on their dogs, and the consequent exhaustion of their powers which must thereby necessarily ensue; and the men calmly await their turn, flogging their charges now and then with impartial indifference whenever they chance to make themselves rather too obnoxious by their whining or their frantic struggles to escape.

Such a plan, however, with highly-strung dogs, is simply suicidal. What with (first) seeing the runners at work, and (secondly) being themselves individually slipped for their spin with strange dogs, why everything conspires to render highly-bred dogs unsteady; and no wonder that in five cases out of ten (if not more) the dogs invariably begin by a mad flush.

Yes, a "mad" flush. They run "fit to break their necks," simply because sense has for the time being deserted them, and they are simply madly wild until they have had their fling and time to cool themselves a bit. No wonder, therefore, that the breakers wish, as often as possible, to go near their dogs. I quite understand that. The matter then remains thus: either train the dogs to work well, even when people and strange dogs are about—a tedious and very costly process, I should imagine, if a small crowd were needed for practice—or else allow the breaker to walk to his charge, so as to counteract the evil influence which the presence of other field-trial goers, their men, and their dogs has upon him.

However, I fancy that—first, if dogs were now and then, when being trained, run with strange dogs and in the presence of strangers; secondly, if, when at public meetings non-runners were not unnecessarily distressed by being allowed to see other dogs work—I fancy that there would be a great deal more steadiness shown then than there is now, especially when the dogs are just slipped.

Concerning the working of field trials by the "heats" plan, I unhesitatingly condemn such a system as decidedly unfair, and I will show it.

First of all I naturally must presume that finding out the best, the second best, and the third best dogs is the object in view where, say, three prizes are given in a stakes. Well, if this is the end in view, I say that by strictly adhering to the heats plan, the judges may (and do) turn out of the stakes dogs that might (and probably would) have taken either second or third prize. Let us suppose, for instance, that at the draw six really crack dogs are so drawn, that they will have to run against each other—and let us suppose that the judges proceed by "points," awarding those points on the whole work done; thus, an absolutely perfect dog should get 100, a bad one 0, an indifferent performer 50, and a fairish dog 75.

Well, now let us suppose that the stake begins with the

three brace of "cracks," A, B, C, D, E, and F. A and B run first; A wins with 90 points; B has only mustered 85. C and D start next; C gets 95 points; D, 90.

E and F go on then; E wins by having 90 points, F only 85.

By these means, anyhow, B, D, and F are out of the stakes, and run no more in it. Let us see now how A, C, and E will fare in the ties, merely premising that the rest of the runners were a lot of indifferent performers, and G, I, K, &c., who have won their heats, only mustered each of them some 50 points.

Now, the running for the first ties begins, and of course as they stand first and next on the card, A and C come first together, when C is put out. Then E beats G easily, and the first ties proceed. In the second ties A of course runs with E. He puts him out, so that A eventually takes the first prize, which is quite correct; but the second and third prizes will have to go to dogs that were not near the perfection of B, C, D, E, or F! And yet some people declare the "heats" plan the *acme* of perfection for deciding field trials!

Well, for the life of me I cannot see it; and I am sincerely grieved—nay, hurt—at seeing good dogs put out of some stakes for the benefit of other dogs not nearly so good as themselves.

Of course I have depicted the case in slightly exaggerated colours purposely to bring my argument into bolder relief. That such things take place no one at all conversant with field trials can deny, and I could give scores of instances to the point. Now I do not call that sort of thing either justice or fair play. It is called justice, to some extent, in this wise: "The best of each brace will compete together"—nothing could be fairer on paper. In practice it is simply shocking, since the *worst* dog of two good dogs may yet be *better* than all the others which run also in the stakes, yet this good dog is put out! Is this fair? Is this just?

"A remedy for the evil?"

Oh! that is easy enough. Add up the points, and give the prizes according to merit—there will be sense in *that*, whereas there is not the shadow of sense in heats.

To put it in another light. Take a trotting meeting run in heats, in which the following results are obtained:

First Heat.		Second Heat.	
A	2.14	D	2.21
B	2.17	E	2.22
C	2.20	F	2.23

For the ties A and D have to run against each other; yet B and C, both put out, have done better time than D! Such a system is simply absurd. It may suit betting-men, who like as many chances of speculation as possible; but it has no *raison d'être* at field trials, where, thank goodness, betting is still unpractised by the professional betting fraternity.

No, the "heats" system is a very good one as regards finding out the very best dog or horse in any given lot; but, as regards the second and third best, it reduces the whole affair to a mere lottery; therefore it is inadmissible, and I really cannot understand how such a plan, so patently and so radically vicious, can possibly have any partisans.

Let the judges run the dogs as they like, singly or in braces; but let them book, or note mentally, the work done by each dog, and let them award the prizes according to the degree of excellence shown individually by the dogs. Any other plan is totally unsatisfactory.

There is another point on which I would beg to draw attention, and it is to the choice of fields.

It is notorious now that certain dogs somehow always get excellent fields for their trials—fields with plenty of room, good laying, excellent cover—and where, therefore, a dog has every chance given him of showing himself to the best advantage; whereas some other dogs, also somehow, are run on bare fallows, with no more covert than a billiard-table, and with bad laying at all times—fields that are narrow and cramped, where fence-breaking is likely to be attempted, as a matter of course, by any dog accustomed to a swinging stride and a good run, and where fur is more likely to be found than feather.

Now, how is this?

No doubt some consider it an excellent joke to palm off a good dog, whose "interest is at a low ebb," into a field where everything is against him, and where the best he can do is to commit no fault, but where pace, nose, ranging, and other qualities are not to be exhibited, there being neither room, nor reason, nor scope to exhibit them. Well, then, why should we see such things? Is it right to have the apportionment of the good fields to be run over left to the choice of individuals? Certainly not. Moreover, a field where no sport is in reason likely to be shown ought to be discarded. Such fields ought to be driven, and the dogs ought to be slipped only where there is a fair chance of discovering game likely to stand the trying process of being found and set to. Now this, I contend, in a bare field is well-nigh an impossibility, and, therefore, running dogs in such places is placing them at a fearful disadvantage. Why not have a rough map of the estate drawn, and the fields numbered ; so that there should be no time lost, no choice left as to favourite fields to anybody, no hesitation on the part of the management as to where to go when a field is done with? As things are now practised, the following is pretty well the invariable formula:

"Keeper!" shouts one of the judges.

No answer. Everybody looking round, and at each other.

"Keeper!" is repeated in a stentorian voice, and with a slight dash of anger.

Everybody squints over the hedge, and somebody ventures to remark that the keeper is not there, which is self-evident and not over-gratifying.

"Then where is he?" the judges inquire still more energetically.

Meanwhile, the cry has been taken up, and "Keeper!" "Keeper!" resounds all round. "Ah! here he is! here he comes!"

The keeper turns up, flushed. Was having his luncheon, is disgusted with the whole affair—can't have one's meal in peace, &c. Finally:

"May it please your lordship," does he say, "do you want me?"

"Of course we do," retorts the now thoroughly riled judge; "we want to know where to go now!"

"Oh, then, this way please, gentlemen."

And we all have to retrace our footsteps! That is a fact. Now no sportsman minds tramping when sport is in question; but going backwards and forwards without rhyme, sense, or reason, simply because a keeper has not always his wits about him, is rather trying. But the case is worse when deliberately we are taken half a mile out of our course in order to secure, for certain dogs, good fields; whereas for other dogs any blessed field will do. Ay, yes, that is a very, very trying sort of business; but as we are all in the dark, more or less, as to the topography and nature of the land, why we follow each other through the gaps like so many sheep, and the farce is played. Now some people notice that sort of thing and groan more or less loudly; but in the field-trial world groaning is allowed *ad libitum*. It is only reform that is not to be hinted at, hence I rather fear I have put "my foot in it" this time; but, as the man said when he placed a canister of gunpowder on the fire, "Anything for a change!"

Why, some people even go the length of actually laughing—yes, positively laughing—at the Kennel Club Grand Prix. Some people really have no respect for even the most sacred things. These most cantankerous of beings say, first, that the running for that prize has no earthly public interest, that it only concerns the members of the Kennel Club, and that no one else takes any interest in it; secondly, they aver that the Kennel Club allows only its members to compete, because they are afraid, if the competition were to be thrown open, that some outsider would carry off that magnificent prize which ought to belong only to a Kennel Club member, &c. &c.

Now it is very rude, to say the least of it, of people to meddle with any particular domestic arrangements. If the Kennel Club members wish to run for their special prize among themselves—literally *en famille*—why should they not? And if they are afraid lest an outsider, if allowed to run, should beat them, why of course it stands to reason that they are acting very wisely in keeping that element of discord away from the scene of action—*ergo*, the Kennel Club is supremely right, and it is to be hoped that those meddling people above referred to will in future "let well alone."

In my next I will conclude all I have to say anent field trials.

THE WORKING OF SPORTING DOGS

AT FIELD TRIALS AND IN THE FIELD.

III.

FROM what I have already stated, it will be seen that, however sterlingly good a dog may be, he is very heavily handicapped for running in a field trial if he belongs to a man who keeps only that one dog (or at most one or two more), simply from the fact that the dog has necessarily been used to single-handed work, or perhaps to work with his only kennel companion, and although perfect in his work when slipped alone or with his chum, yet, when matched at the trials with a newcomer, he throws for the time being his breaking to the winds, makes up his mind not to be out-run, and thus puts himself out. This is so well known to the cognoscenti, that it seems rather curious, to say the least, that the "match" plan for trying pointers and setters in public should be in vogue at all. In private no such thing occurs. For instance, when a dog is to be tried in private, say before an intending purchaser, the seller will either run his dog alone, or with a kennel companion; but he certainly would not allow his dog to be tried with a strange dog, because he knows very well that, whether the strange dog be wild or no, he will make his own dog quite unlike his usual self. Well, this being so well known, is it not wonderful that the "match" plan should be resorted to at field trials? Of course, in large kennels the dogs may be and are run alternately together, so that when they are individually slipped with strange dogs in actual field trials, they pay but little or absolutely no attention to the fact that they have rivals, being, so to speak, used to that sort of thing; hence the countenance given to the "match" system by the owners of large kennels. But, as I have pointed out, the man with only one or a brace of dogs will be grievously handicapped as long as such a system obtains, and it stands to reason that he must be so.

Edward Armstrong—than whom few men have had better success at field trials—is a strong partisan of the "match" plan. Why? Simply, I presume, just because he has a large kennel under his management, runs his dogs constantly together, matching them ever with different runners, and thus ensures their perfect or almost perfect indifference to whatever dogs they may chance to be slipped with. Edward Armstrong is perfectly correct in his views, though he must admit that virtually, by the very fact of his being able to match his intended field-trial runners in private, with many dogs if he chose, he obtains a great "pull" over the man who, owning only two or three dogs, can effect but little diversion in their matching. There is no doubt that such is the case, and to give a strong instance to the point, I would beg to refer my readers to the working of Bang and Mike, both formerly Mr. Samuel Price's pointers. The two dogs, when working together, were admirably perfect. Slipped individually with strange dogs, Bang, owing to his greater experience, just held his own, but Mike dropped considerably. In fact, the latter, after changing hands last year, ran a brute, and many strangers thought he was not, and never had been, broken. I knew better, having seen him in his prime, when in the braces at Shrewsbury he, with his father Bang, did such wonderful work. I was the first then to predict their success to Mr. Price. "They will take first prize," I said, when, standing by the hedge, I was taking my notes, and Mr. Price was picking up his dogs. "Do you think so?" said he. "I am sure of it," I replied. And they did.

But at Horseheath last year what a change in Mike! He was then Mr. Salter's property, and whether the change of masters had upset him, or whether he had been neglected, I know not; but he ran wildly, and totally unlike his former self. And the same may be said of the same gentleman's little black-and-white-ticked pointer bitch Romp. Romp. two years ago, when Mr. Bartram ran her, was a clinker. She went at an incredible pace, was gifted with a wonderful nose, and was admirably broken. When she ran last year she went like a wild thing, and astonished everybody, including myself, who expected great things of her, particularly because I knew her to be endowed with a very independent temperament. She would, two years ago, take her own line, pay no attention to anybody, go like a shot, and find the birds whilst some of her rivals had hardly done turning round a mangold-wurzel or a turnip. Last year she also took her own line—but alas! a wrong one—went away right ahead, broke fence, flushed, &c., and ran as wildly as possibly could be.

Now this bad working of Mike and Romp (since I took

them as instances) I ascribe mostly to their being matched with strange dogs, although the change of breaker may have something to do with it; anyhow, matching strange setting dogs together is anything but conducive to first-rate sport. Then why should it be done?

It always makes a true sportsman riled to see a dog that he knows to be a good one thus being made a fool of through his otherwise very praiseworthy spirit of emulation.

Don't tell me that matching them thus makes the dogs spin faster. It does so only at first. A really good dog, at all times, goes at the utmost speed he can keep up. It is natural in him that he should. He is as anxious as you, the sportsman, to find birds, and that speedily too, and therefore he goes as though his very life depended on his speed. That is my experience of A 1 dogs. No matter whether they are alone or with a companion, they go "express," and only stop when they drop from sheer exhaustion. Ay, I have seen some dogs panting on the ground, gasping for breath, and likely to die, when, being out of condition, they had tried to do that which their instinct had prompted them to do, but which their want of condition forbade. I do not for a moment wish to deny that, when first slipped, two strange dogs tear away faster than if slipped alone; but that sort of gallop is *à la* greyhound, with head low and stern high—a mad gallop in the setting dog, and one which is totally incompatible with his working well, because setting dogs must be cool and collected, and the sportsman who is used to them knows that, when extended and at speed for useful work, the dogs go level, and in a sweeping, graceful manner which is perfectly characteristic, with their heads always turned to the breeze to catch scent, and they are above all thoroughly intent upon *that*; whereas the mad gallopers who tear away to spite each other don't care for scent—they glare at each other, and only mean racing, not work, and that is not as it should be. Well, then, since this is acknowledged as a patent fact, why should such a plan be adhered to? When, after a trial last year, an owner, in the course of conversation, told me, "My dog was beaten deservedly, for he ran wild here, but you should just see him at home along with me!" I could not help smiling; and had I previously known the circumstances of owner and dog, I could have predicted the failure beforehand. In fact, owners neglect far too much preparing their dogs for work with strange dogs in actual trials; and those whose keepers can and do so prepare them have always an enormous advantage over the others.

Now the thing is this: Is it a desideratum that a setter or pointer should work absolutely and equally well when alone, or with his usual chum, or when slipped with a strange dog? To this I certainly say yes, for it may be some day desirable to work the dog with strange dogs; but it is not a *sine quâ non*; and if a man only wants one single-handed dog, he must not judge from the results of any field trial that a given dog is unfit for his purpose. The dog may be, as his owner justly states, absolutely perfect when working alone or with a dog he knows, and yet be nowhere with strangers. Hence, no doubt, by the system actually pursued at field trials of matching the dogs *à la* greyhound, we do not see the best work that can be performed by all the dogs, and many a good dog is put out merely because he gets out of tune when called upon to perform that which he is not used to do, and to which he has the greatest antipathy; for all strange setting dogs at first sight are jealous, and run jealous of each other, and jealousy won't do when a cool head and a cool "nose" are absolutely necessary to success. Therefore, the man of moderate means, if he enters only one dog and wishes for success, ought to have that dog used to any companions; but it would be better for such a man to compete only in braces, when, by running, say, his only two dogs always together, he will find that they will work with him anywhere as well as at home, and if they were perfect there, they will be so at the trials; whereas a single dog will be likely to go "all to pieces" (and that is rather disheartening), unless he were worked single-handed.

But there are now no stakes provided for single-handed work—the more the pity, say I; for I know for a fact that, were such stakes run for at field trials, many sportsmen would attend or enter who now do not, because they require or own only single-handed dogs; but, as the trials are now conducted, they cannot see or show the dogs to their best advantage, and therefore do not attend; and that is the plain truth, however strange it may appear.

In short, I, in common with many other sportsmen, would wish field trials to be more thoroughly open to, and patronised by, the public than they now are. They are open to all, I know, but *de facto* but few comparatively care or are able to run dogs at them now; and hence a sort of field-trial world has been created—very nice in its little way, but not sufficiently broad in its principles to induce the public to swell its ranks. I would like to see all sportsmen (throughout the British kingdom or the world) who own really good dogs looking forward to running these dogs at our public trials; but that end will never be attained unless reform steps in, and new arrangements are made, whereby every facility will be given to owners to show their dogs in their true colours; and to this end I think that field trials taking place during the shooting season would be the only real test. For puppies the usual spring meetings would be, of course, desirable; but there is no doubt that spring meetings for "made" dogs are mere farces; and these dogs come to look upon them as most excellent jokes—witness Mr. Barclay Field's old setter Dick, who jumped after a partridge that rose on his point and very nearly gobbled it up, at Shrewsbury last year. Evidently Dick thought that, since no game ever did fall to the gun, he had better join in, and try what he could do in the way of filling the bag, which was very sensible on his part—very!

Well, now, would anyone believe that in private there are some sportsmen who do not seem to be aware of those causes which may and do affect the working of sporting dogs? Hence the very strange and contradictory statements one may hear about a given dog—say, respectively, by his buyer and his seller. According to the latter the dog is perfect; whereas, if the former is to be believed, an ounce of shot ought to be his reward; "he is a brute totally unbroken," &c. Instances of that sort of thing I could give by the hundred. For instance, had Mike or Romp been sent last year anywhere—to a stranger, say, on trial —and they had behaved with him as they did at the trials, why the stranger would certainly have declared the dogs never to have been broken. "Wild, you know; never were trained, in fact." And thus the question would have been settled to his satisfaction, no doubt; whereas everybody knows that this dog and bitch have been A 1 in their day, and probably will be so again with a little trouble.

The moral of this is, don't let your dog be tried either by strangers or with strange dogs, or to a certainty he will make a fool of himself, at first; therefore, either in public or in private, anything of that sort ought to be avoided as far as possible. And as regards private trials of sporting dogs, one of the most unpleasant features of the system of sending dogs on trial lies in the fact that not only are the dogs so sent very heavily handicapped by the very circumstances of their trials (new masters, new faces, new ground, and strange dogs), but in nine cases out of ten the men who try them do not know what they are about, and take no trouble in the matter, but put the blame on the dogs. Even keepers, who by trade ought to know all about dogs, are getting wofully deficient in that respect. Of course, there are some very clever keepers, to whom dog-breaking and dog-working have no secrets; but these few men will know that I am right as regards the remainder of their brethren.

Owing to the now prevalent systems of battueing and driving, the rising gamekeeper-of-the-period has a retriever peculiarly broken for his own use, and that is the only dog he cares for. Give him a brace of pointers or setters to try, and he is all at sea. He swears at them if they get beyond fifty yards from him, declares that they will flush everything, and tells his master that they are no good. And even in retrievers (which breed one might think would be his *forte*) this rising star is as completely in the dark as can be, in ten cases out of a dozen.

Let a master send a perfect retriever to such a man to

try, and this is how he proceeds: He leaves the dog in charge of a boy all day whilst the shooting is going on, and, when it is over, he takes the dog in hand, and tells him to "Seek dead." In short, he uses him as a keeper's dog. Well, the dog picks up thus say a dozen birds, and the consequence is that in future he will, when sent on, be always on the look-out for more than one bird, and give no end of trouble to his user.

Another sort of keeper, who is commissioned to kill game for his master, uses the perfect retriever sent on trial as follows: He is a good shot, and looks more for the "pot" than for the sport; hence, as soon as he fires, he calls out at every shot, "Go on! Fetch him up! Hie, lost!" &c., and thus he causes the dog to run in to shot. Besides this, as likely as not he will use the dog to bolt a rabbit from a hedge now and then, and as a matter of fact he ruins the dog for ever. There are many such so-called keepers abroad, and, the tendency of the age being to resort more to mechanical means in order to find game than to the subtle and delightful working of dogs, as a natural sequence the rising generation of keepers grows to be A 1 in breeding and rearing game, they are capital drill-sergeants for their squads of beaters, but they are getting wofully behindhand in any knowledge of sporting dogs, their working, and their qualities.

Now any fool can drive clodhoppers through a wood, or order his wife and daughters to feed the young broods; but it requires a *bonâ-fide* sporting education in a keeper to enable him to know and to work a good dog; and I contend that, unfortunately, many of the new class of keepers know absolutely nothing about the latter. But for that their masters are to blame. They would like to cram ten thousand birds in a covert, have them driven to them by an army into a corner, kill as many as they can, sitting down on a chair and smoking their pipes all the while—and they call it sport! Well, they may if they like; but, for the life of me, I can't see any sport in it, and that is the plain truth. A waste of sport, I call it; for, consider, with good dogs, what fun one could have had with many of these birds when they were all dispersed in their haunts! Yes, it is a dreadful waste of good stuff. Of course people can do what they like with their own, but they must not really call that sort of thing sport. When and where does the sport come in? In short, shooting game, when deprived of the search for the game with dogs, is no longer shooting—it is "killing birds with a gun;" it is not that glorious pastime to which our ancestors gave the name of "shooting;" and were I to give up seeing my dogs searching for my game, I would hang up my guns forever, for killing the birds, without having the ineffable pleasure of seeing my dogs find them one after the other, would have no charm whatsoever for me; and I know many true sportsmen who agree with me there. No dogs, no sport—that is my motto. Shooting without searching for one's game, in my humble opinion, is not, never has been, and never will be sport; and those who call it sport do so merely as a flower of rhetoric, since there is nothing in it that can warrant the appellation. It is good fun, but not sport, since glass beads or air bladders would answer the purpose quite as well.

THE WORKING OF SPORTING DOGS

AT FIELD TRIALS AND IN THE FIELD.

IV.

As it appears that I have been misunderstood on sundry points in my previous arguments, I will refer to them in the course of this chapter, so as to render my meaning perfectly intelligible.

In training, I would always advise the dogs to remain dropped until their breaker comes to them; and the reason for this is too obvious to need enlarging upon. But when once the dogs are thoroughly broken, and have given up their youthful vagaries—in short, when they are thoroughly up to their business—I deprecate this protracted dropping in private work, for the also very obvious reason that it is sickening to a private gentleman sportsman to have to go to each of his dogs before they resume their quartering; and, however much this may be allowable at public field trials (where steadying the dogs is desirable on account of the manifold temptations to riot which are then in their way), it stands to reason that in private no sportsman would look upon that sort of thing as a desirable feature if he wants the dogs for work, not for show. Of course, if a private sportsman gets a brace of dogs so broken, and, just to show them to friends, likes them to stick to their former breaking, in order to produce an effect (which it rarely fails to do)—well, he can if he likes; but no man of means in his senses would deliberately bind himself to work dogs in that style throughout the whole sporting season, because such dire labour and loss of time would thus be entailed on him, that he would soon give up the style if he only wanted the dogs for himself. At field trials the case is different. The higher the breaking, the better the chances of the dogs being noticed; and it is sometimes there a necessity for perfect work that the dog should at all times be walked to.

Someone said that I suggested the training of young dogs in the presence of strangers.

I did nothing of the sort; I suggest accustoming young dogs (when they are broken) to the presence of strangers, which makes a considerable difference. And I advise this simply because, if the dogs have never seen anyone but their breaker in the field, they are sure to go amiss at a field trial when in the presence of a crowd.

Mr. Bartram deprecated the sentence "running fit to break their necks," and seems to think that I do not like pace. Had he read my first and last chapters he would see that, on the contrary, I am a partisan of pace. What I dislike to see is "wild" running, as that occasioned at first by the matching of two strange dogs.

As to the "heats" plan, I stick to my opinion that it is an abominably vicious plan. Mr. Bartram, however, declares that he prefers that plan, but, oddly enough, he says: "It seems to me clear as daylight that the best dog, bar accident, will win, and that the second best may be run out!" Yet he advocates that system, and wonders that I call it radically vicious! Why, it is so much so that no man, except he likes luck to play a part in the affair, or else for the fun of the thing, would run dogs under such conditions. Had I the best dogs (for argument sake) in the world, I would not run them on those terms, because I dislike and object to elements of luck in an affair where no opening ought to be left for luck. Let worth win, say I, and hang luck! But to acknowledge deliberately, as Mr. Bartram does, that the second best dogs may be put out—by no fault of theirs, but merely because the judges find it easier to put them out than to book or remember their work—and yet to profess a liking for the system is simply slightly staggering; and it is not likely that the public at large will ever be made to indorse implicitly such field-trial results. This being so, I am right in denouncing the plan as vicious. If it were an impossibility for the judges to remember the work of the dogs, I could understand the desirability of concentrating their attention to each brace, and of putting out the worst of each two runners, and running the best of each brace against each other; but does Mr. Bartram mean to tell me that from his notes he could not tell the best four or five dogs, even in a twenty-dog stake? Of course he could. Well, then, if he can do it, others can. Nay, it has been done; and I have seen it done most admirably at Shrewsbury.

Of course, people will differ, especially when their interests are at stake; but what I contend is this. Here are two plans: one, the "heats" plan, which avowedly is most unsatisfactory, and inevitably so; the other, by which the judges pronounce as to the respective merits of the dogs, and award the prizes accordingly. Now, which is the most rational?

Of course, someone will argue that the judges are not infallible. But then this will apply also to their decisions by the "heats" plan; and therefore, so far, the objection is equally applicable to both plans; but anyhow, by allowing the judges to award according to merit, one has only to contend against their mistakes of judgment—and these mistakes, be it borne in mind, are only problematical—whereas by the "heats" system, not only are similar problematical mistakes in the judging as likely to arise, but the system itself is moreover absolutely certain to put out good dogs. This being so, of two evils choose the least, say I, and adopt the plan which is likely to give the best results.

This, however, does not suit a certain section of the field-trial world, who accept judges, and then never fail to deprecate their awards if their dogs are left out in the cold. It is a strange thing, but true, that some owners look upon it as an insult, direct or otherwise, or else as plain proof of incapacity on the part of the judges, if they do not endorse these owners' opinions that their dogs are the best. Now, it is notorious that, of all persons present, such susceptible owners are the least able, at the actual trial of their dogs, to form a correct judgment of their performances.

The excitement of the trial on its intrinsic merits, added perhaps also to a slight dose of spite against the rival owner (such a thing as spite is known, and very well known indeed, in the field-trial world), then a bit of self-pride, together with the spirit of interested, and therefore jealous, ownership—everything tends to place such owners at a disadvantage in respect to impartially deciding which of the dogs, theirs or their rivals', ran the best.

Hence the very entertaining remarks one hears now and then by these sportsmen, or their men, as to quite imaginary faults committed by their obnoxious rivals' dogs, and their total oblivion of the patent shortcomings of their own. How often have I not heard a competitor, or breaker, bitterly or sarcastically complain that he did not see why his dog was put out. "But he flushed," or "chased" (as the case might be), someone would reply.

"Nothing of the sort," would the owner or breaker retort angrily; "the other dog ran into any number of birds; and he won't back; he does not point steadily; he drops badly," &c., when just the reverse had been the case. In such matters, owners' or breakers' spectacles evidently place a man at an immense disadvantage. Of course there are cases when complaints are but too well founded; but these are, as a rule, pointed out by the press. Still it must be admitted that a reporter cannot always, and in every case, see every nicety in the working of two dogs, and when two crack workers chance to run together, a very slight thing will often turn the balance; and this slight thing may have taken place over accidental ground, where the view was now and then interrupted, and when therefore necessarily a break must have occurred in one's *de visu* notes of the trial.

However, I should deprecate much any judgment which happens to be founded on a slight basis, because that sort of thing is very unsatisfactory. When a dog has made absolutely no mistake, but, on the contrary, has distinguished himself, and is put out simply because the other dog, in a given time, has found one brace more than he, for instance; then I say that such a decision is very unfair to the so-called beaten dog, since probably, with another run, he might have reversed the tables. Now some judges seem to have decided leanings towards certain dogs; and it actually looks as though they run them on and on until that sort of thing takes place, when they have thus a shadow of a pretence to award in their favour. That sort of thing, if I am correct in my views, is not right; nevertheless, there may have been no intention in the matter, merely a bias. Then unbiassed judges ought to be chosen.

The remark that as I have not been directly interested in field-trial matters I cannot judge of their merits is wrong in principle. He who stands by is better able to judge of the blows given in a fight than the combatants themselves. And so it is in every contest where self-interest is necessarily at stake among the competitors. They don't see half what is to be seen; those who look on, and who are totally disinterested and unbiassed in the matter, can best form a judgment. Such is my opinion, at any rate.

Now I have always loved sporting dogs; I think them marvellously admirable animals; therefore I have always a penchant to favour them rather. But, like all sportsmen, I have an innate craving for perfection in work, and by that severe standard unconsciously I judge all the dogs I see; and being, at field trials, in no wise directly interested in the success of any of the runners, I think that I and those similarly situated, for that very reason, stand a far better chance of coming to a right decision respecting the dogs' respective merits than the majority of the owners or breakers themselves. Not that I claim a knowledge by any means superior to that of these owners (most field-trial men are second to none in their sporting qualifications); but I contend that, involuntarily, self-interest will now and then affect more or less the independence of their judgment when comparing the relative merits of strange dogs with their own.

There are, however, several owners who seem totally unaffected by anything of the sort. They look on with the most admirable and praiseworthy impartiality, and will say, even before the flag is sent up: "Well, I know I am out this time;" and they are. But there are many others who always grumble; *ergo*, the few that form the exception only prove the rule that it is difficult for the majority of owners to judge impartially of the work that has been done when their dogs were actually engaged in the contest.

Respecting the working of field trials, I can see but one objection to the dogs being tried singly, and it is that, in order to judge about backing, eventually the dogs would have to be tried in braces, which perhaps would be awkward.

But anyhow, whether the dogs were worked singly or in braces, as soon as a dog makes a deliberate mistake let him be put out, since he would have no chance of figuring in the prize list. This would save time; and if the dogs were working in braces, and the turned-out dog had misbehaved at the beginning of his trial, let another dog be called to work in his place with the one left in, until the latter, or the newcomer, or both, have shown sufficiently good work to warrant being stopped for good, or for an eventual direct trial with another or other good dogs similarly circumstanced. If both dogs misbehave themselves, turn both out. This would be another great saving of time, which does not occur in the "heats" plan, where one will find that the best of two indifferent dogs who has been declared the winner of a heat is again brought out to run with another dog in the ties; and, although by rights the indifferent performer ought not to have a shadow of a chance of winning, yet he is run again, and if the really good dogs in the stakes have put each other out, this brute actually may figure in the prize list, thus wasting the time of the public, and, into the bargain, crowning his infamy by robbing other more worthy dogs of their laurels!

To resume then the plan I would like to see carried out: If two good rival dogs ran together, and were as near perfection as could be, both flags ought to be sent up, as an intimation that a favourable estimation having been made of their work, they both stood a chance of taking a prize. The objection that, as the dogs have not all been working in the same fields and under the same circumstances, therefore their comparative work cannot be estimated, is not of any vital importance. If the dogs are all treated alike, and are allotted fair fields to work in, there is no reason why they should not show themselves in their true colours, and these will readily be appreciated by the judges, who, taking perfection as the standard test, will readily be able to pick out the wheat from the chaff.

The fact is, bad scent in many cases is synonymous with "dogs with no nose," or unbroken, and the proof of this is—what I have often noticed—after some dogs have been flushing repeatedly, through bad scent, of course, there comes one or a brace of dogs who are A 1 in their work, and these perform admirably. The next brace perhaps flush; but the next again, good ones, don't. Well, it is very handy, in the face of a failure, to be able to fall back on the want of scent. But how is it that all the dogs are not so affected?

Field-trial judges are men of experience in sporting matters, they know how to use their judgment in all cases, and they do not allow their judgment to be overridden by facts. Thus, if a dog commits an involuntary flush, such as when the birds see him, or if they are below him and he cannot possibly scent them, why should he be penalised? One might just as well punish him for not being able to shoot the birds. But if, with the wind in his favour, and in good covert, the dog deliberately turns to the scent, draws, and flushes, then I say "out he ought to be;" and there would be an end of him at once anyhow. But the judges must decide which is which; and they do it right well, as a rule, so that the real value of the dogs is arrived at.

By-the-way, the driving of fields I alluded to did not relate to fallows, &c., only, but especially to those very bare grass and wheat fields where some dogs are now and then slipped, but where they ought not to be so run, by reason of the covert being really too thin and too bare there to afford anything like reliable lying for the birds. Such fields ought to be driven as well as the ploughed land, &c., and not worked over.

As to arguing that there is in field trials no absolute (*i.e.* mechanical) test, it does not prove *per se* that the test used is not in its way as reliable as clockwork. The test is mental, and is PERFECTION, and by it anything may be judged by an impartial and well-trained mind with tolerably excellent accuracy. The thing is to get the man of impartial and well-trained mind, who, accepting the facts as facts, but weighing them according to his judgment, grants to each dog his right number of points for his work, and is eventually enabled to judge of the relative merits of all the dogs with pretty near as much certainty and accuracy as if each of them had been running a race against time. Should there have been such a level in quality shown by two or three dogs in separate trials as to make dividing them a matter of some difficulty, these dogs could divide, or, if time allowed, they could be run among themselves for actual comparison if desirable. I, at any rate, see no insuperable difficulties in all this, but quite the reverse—a most satisfactory and plain way of settling a much-vexed question; of putting an end to that detestable element of luck which virtually makes the draw in the "heats" plan a matter of tossing for honours, and of doing away with that abominable systematically countenanced fluking which places indifferent performers in the prize list over the heads of dogs which are far better than themselves. In short, as I said before, we want sterling worth to win, and not lucky incompetence. And since by the "heats" plan some of the best dogs must fatally be put out, I say—down with it. Any plan is better than one whose only (and then doubtful) claim is that it makes the work of judging more easy. If a judge of working dogs cannot among twenty dogs pick out the three or four or five best, and work them together for finally deciding which will take the prizes, then all I can say is, I would not give much for his judgment.

It would not speak much for his intellectual powers if, with his notes deliberately taken before him, he cannot come to a satisfactory settlement of the awards, but must needs resort to such barbarous and primitive means as the "heats" plan enforces. Such means were, no doubt, resorted to when people could not read or write—before the Flood—because they were so easy of application, and it relieved the judge of all thought and all responsibility; but they are inadmissible now. The number of dogs in any stake at a field trial is not so great that the reporters' notes cannot show the work of each; therefore, the judges can also take notes or book comparative numbers, and judge accordingly.

I have only to say about coursing, wrestling, &c., where the "heats" plan is resorted to, that if coursers, wrestlers, &c. are content to enter into a sort of lottery, that is no reason why field-trialers should. Moreover, there are, in coursing and in wrestling, &c., so many elements of luck that, virtually, one more or less does not signify; but in field-trial work the luck element ought to be reduced to its minimum; and since a pretty correct estimate can be formed of all the dogs, why not place them according to that estimate?

If this is not more generally done, it is not because the system is not intrinsically the best, but simply because the majority of the competitors somehow seem to have no wish to trust blindly to the judges' decisions, and therefore they bind the judges by the "heats" rules; although by so binding the judges, the competitors ought to be, and are, aware, that they provide a remedy worse than the disease. However, there the fact remains, that many of them would rather run the *certain* risk of losing by chance, than that of *problematically* losing only by the fiat of the judges; because in the first case allowances will be made for the defective system which allows luck to play so prominent a part in the awards, whereas in the other the judges' decisions always have weight with outsiders, and therefore the losing owners take their reverses to heart, and, wrongly or rightly, accuse the judges of partiality. That is not a healthy state of things for a sport to be in, if that is why "heats" rules are stuck to so persistently.

I must apologise to Mr. Bartram if I have in any way infringed on any notion of his. The idea of having plans of the estates was freely discussed at Shrewsbury three or four years ago, to my knowledge.

A correspondent agrees with me in the desirability of having stakes for braces, since the best work to be seen is shown in those stakes. He also advocates stakes for amateurs, which is a likely notion; but he is rather severe in his remarks about the breakers. How can they "try every dodge to disconcert and circumvent the amateur"? Dodges would not be allowed (if complained of) were they tried; but this is not likely to be the case with, on the whole, a very highly respectable body of men, whose talents in their line are simply admirable.

In *The Field*, of Feb. 23, Mr. Bartram says that the dog who can work well with another dog is preferable to one who will not do so. This is such a patent truism that no one can dream of going against it. What I contended was that, for the man with a small kennel, it was next to impossible to produce a dog that would run well with any strange dog; *ergo*, the small-kennel owner was placed at a disadvantage; *ergo*, for such a man, running the dog singly would be preferable. And many sportsmen who work dogs singly would like to patronise stakes for such single-handed work. The same argument holds good for the small-kennel owner who owns a good brace. Why should not he show them, since they exhibit absolute perfection?

Mr. Bartram adds that, "by matching the dogs we see all their defects," thus backing my own views unconsciously.

But he gives us a rider, "that this exhibition of defects is of great advantage to breeders." That may be; but surely, *primâ facie*, a man who runs his dogs at a field trial, wants to win the trial, and therefore, anything that puts his dogs out of form is not welcome to him, at any rate; *ergo*, matching strange dogs is unsatisfactory work for field trials. Never mind the after considerations—we are only considering actual work just now—and it strikes me that it is uncommonly hard on a man to make him pay an entry fee of five or more guineas for the privilege of letting his dogs make fools of themselves in public, for the exclusive benefit of breeders!

I have been gratified beyond measure at finding that Mr. Samuel Price was endorsing my views, because I know him to be a most liberal and clear-minded man, perfectly untrammelled by clique notions or conventionalities, and his opinion is therefore entitled to the genuine consideration of all who are interested in the subject. Respecting his severe strictures on Mike and Romp's new keeper, I should like to say a word. Knoulton is a really painstaking man, and I am sure Mr. Samuel Price would be the very last man in the world to blame him did he know the truth. Well, Knoulton told me that both Mike and Romp had been in his charge such a very short time, that they did not know him; and this appeared certainly to be the case, as both disregarded either his call or whistle, and seemed to be looking for someone else. Therefore I think that Knoulton ought to be held blameless in the matter.

In a number of *The Field*, "Glenwood" says that with my views as to the unsatisfactory results arrived at by the "heats" plan, both Mr. Bartram and Mr. Samuel Price agree, but that both are unanimous in rejecting my suggestions.

Working of Sporting Dogs.

Mr. Samuel Price does not reject my suggestions; on the contrary, he states that he prefers, with me, the Shrewsbury system. "Glenwood's" plan — to find the second dog exclusively from amongst those beaten by the first-prize taker — would be most unsatisfactory. For instance, dogs Nos. 4, 6, 8, 10, 12, 14, and 16, which were beaten in the first round, might be all of them superior to No. 2; yet No. 2 would run for second prize, whereas 4, 6, 8, 10, 12, 14, and 16 would not!

And the same holds good for first ties. 7, 11, 15 might be better dogs than 3, yet they would be out of it; whereas 3 would run again, and this merely because he had chanced to run against No. 1! "Glenwood" will at once perceive the unsatisfactory character of his proposal. So I think I am absolutely justified in saying that the only satisfactory plan is that of placing each dog according to his work, irrespective of any mechanical rule which could put him out.

As regards battues, I never denied that they are "enjoyed" by sportsmen. I suppose they do enjoy them, since they join in them. But I can't see what there is to enjoy, beyond the killing practice, which is good fun for a little while. I have tried it, and invariably got literally tired of it, after an hour's time. Because good sportsmen join in battues, it does not prove them to be "sport." Where is in it that "sporting craft" which makes of a shooter a sportsman? And then, look at the cold-blooded cruelty of knocking over many birds, and actually waiting to pick them up until the beaters are out! Poor birds! what have they done to be made to suffer such tortures? If a sportsman gets only an insignificant sore heel, he winces and groans all day. What would he say if he had two or three shots in his bowels, together with a broken thigh or arm, and was left to pant on the ground whilst the shooters are laughing and enjoying themselves, regardless of the state he is in?

No. A state of affairs which countenances such unspeakable horrors is not, never has been, and never will deserve the noble appellation of "sport." The last time I was at a battue I broke a hare's back; it squeaked terribly as it ran into a net and I put my gun down and went to kill it, in spite of my friends' entreaties to the contrary, for I could not stand to hear the poor animal's cries, and had I allowed it to suffer whilst I was finishing the *bouquet*, I should have felt ashamed of myself. No; a thousand times, no! A piece of "entertainment" which covers the ground with maimed and unspeakably-suffering birds is not sport, and I protest against such a name being given to a pretentious, cruelly cold-blooded, and totally uncalled-for expedient.

If anyone can show me sport in it, I am ready to listen to arguments; but I have tried it, and weighed it, and found it wanting in all the elements of sport.

A DAY'S WILDFOWLING ON THE ORWELL.

I WAS rather unfortunate on that day, a terrific hailstorm overcoming us just in the nick of time, and so bad was the river then that we had (much against my wishes) to put back rather early to Ipswich. But to begin at the beginning. I started by the 7.30 A.M. train from Liverpool Street; and my readers will well imagine my grief when, at about eight o'clock, I perceived that it was raining. "Hard lines!" thought I; "but I am now in for it, and will stick to it, cost what may." Still, it was not a pleasant look-out by any means.

When the train arrived at Manningtree, I glanced curiously over the marsh. The tide was low, the flats were bare, and I saw with pleasure, in the far distance, a few large waders on the feed.

Onwards again, and we soon got to Ipswich. I took a fly at once, and drove to the harbour—about a quarter of a mile off—engaged a waterman, got my gun, ammunition, and a flask aboard, and away we went. By Jove! how cold it was! And did not the wind blow, that's all! To windward the sky was of that leaden hue so portentous of rain or snow, and I volunteered, as I sat shivering on the stern-sheets, the remark that in all likelihood we should get a good ducking ere the day was over.

"Should not wonder, sir," said my man; "it do look bad yonder!"

As soon as we were clear of the few ships in the river, I took the big gun out of its cover and went to sit forward, arranging my cartridge-bag handy by my side.

"You see," I remarked to the waterman, "I shall be better able to fire from this post of vantage. But will the boat be easy to manage, being thus put out of trim?"

"Well, we will try, anyhow," said he; "and I daresay I will manage."

I then twisted the thick gun-cover around my ankles to keep my feet warm. I buttoned up my ulster over my knees, and henceforth I was "all eyes" forward.

"Seen any birds about lately?" queried I.

"Pretty few. Mostly curloos and oxbirds," said he. "The best part of the river, however, is by the wood, on your right. There you will be sure to see some presently."

I got, then, my "Dollond" out, and scanned the flats on both sides, and soon I perceived a flock of small waders on our starboard. They were feeding on the mud, and were about a hundred and thirty yards from us.

"Shall I fire at them?"

"Well," said my companion, "of course, sir, you know best if your gun will carry that distance. They be a precious long way off, anyhow."

"I don't mean that," I said. "The gun, I know, will kill some, even farther than that; but I want to know if we could get the birds, supposing I killed some of them?"

"Oh yes; let us see," said he, turning round. "Yes;

there is a bit of hard mud lower down, where I could land, and I daresay I could get to the place where they are."

"Right you are! Then head straight for them, and I will get ready."

He pulled with a will; but we got stuck within thirty yards of the flat.

"No matter," I said, "I will have a try." Saying these words, I cocked the gun, rose quietly, took a deliberate aim, let fly—and was nearly knocked overboard.

"The deuce!" exclaimed I, ruefully. "What is the matter now?"

"She did kick, and no mistake," remarked my companion, who was taking a very lively interest in my proceedings.

"Ay, that she did," rejoined I, rubbing my right arm with a wince. "I suppose I did not shoulder it properly. Better luck next time. But—any birds killed?"

"Dunno, sir. Saw a lot going away."

"Hand me the glass," said I, "I may as well have a look." I got on the spot at once. There were three birds stark dead.

"Pull away," cried I, "and land. You will find them all of a lump, close together."

We had a job to get clear of the mud; but once fairly floated, rowing to the "hard" was easy enough. Landing, however, was not so easy, as, do all we could, the boat would not get near enough for a dry landing. I did not feel inclined for a footbath; but my fellow did not mind.

"I will go, master," said he.

"Right," said I; "you shall have a glass of brandy when you come back, to prevent you from taking cold."

He laughed, and overboard he went, splashing away

merrily. In a minute or so he was back with four birds, all ring-plovers. "You only could see three," said the man, "because t'other one was in a hole. There is another one running away, but I can't go after him."

Well, he stepped aboard, and we shoved her off. Scarcely were we under weigh than a tremendous downpour of rain came on our devoted heads; the wind roared, the sea rose, and the squall was, altogether, surprising. In the midst of it a wood-pigeon came by at a great height and at a terrific pace. I put the gun up at him at once, but I somehow dreaded the recoil, and accordingly missed the bird. The recoil, however, was not nearly so bad as at first, but the "ringing" of the gun made my fingers tingle.

"I must do something to these cartridges," I thought. "The gun is too light for them; that is what it is."

I accordingly opened one with my knife, and withdrew about a quarter of an ounce of shot or so, closed the case again, and loaded the gun with it.

This done, and whilst keeping my "weather eye" about, I doctored a few more cartridges in the same manner ready for use, and then I felt satisfied that an improvement would thus be effected. In the midst of this occupation a boat, propelled by two oarsmen, and with a shooter seated astern, passed us. The sportsman looked very business-like, with his thick coat and fur cap, and his double gun appeared to be one of a decent bore. He fired soon after at oxbirds, as far as I could judge, but the mist and rain were so thick that there was no deciding for certain what the birds were from where we stood. The wind by that time had worked itself into a regular gale.

"Methinks we would do well to follow this sportsman's example," I remarked to my oarsman.

"Go back to harbour, you mean, sir?"

"Yes. I think there won't be much to be done to-day. It is so squally that there is hardly any firing possible, the boat rocks about so, and the rain is so persistent that it will be dark very soon. Anyhow we will go as far as the Hall, and no farther."

Accordingly we went. We found no birds whatsoever on the shores, beyond seagulls, crows, and oxbirds; the latter out of range. We were just going to turn her head back, and I was sincerely disgusted with the absence of sport, when what should I see but two ducks coming from over the Orwell Park, on the other shore, right on to us.

"Easy!" whispered I, seizing the gun. "Easy, here are two birds coming!"

The man dropped his oars alongside, and we both crouched in the boat. At the rate of fifty or sixty miles an hour, the birds came with a regular swift motion of their pinions, and, as straight as could be, they flew towards the boat. As soon as they were within range I jumped up. The birds swerved at this movement, but boom! went my 2½ oz. of No. 1 shot, and, hurrah! both came down! One quite dead—the drake. The duck is only winged, however, and she settles within a hundred and fifty yards of us, on the sea.

"Pull! pull!" I cry enthusiastically. I load, and help my man, and we row with desperation. When we are within fifty yards, I see at a glance that the bird is a very lively cripple.

"I will give it a barrel, to make sure," says I.

"Do!" says the man, who was quite as excited as I was.

I cock the hammer, shoulder the gun, squint along the tube, and was pulling, when lo! there was no bird to be seen! "Hang ye!" exclaimed I, vexed at the bird's tactics.

"What's the row?" queried the sailor.

"Gone to the bottom—dived. Let us look out for her now."

We both stood up among the angry billows, and a nice stiffish job we found it to be, too. Banged about from side to side—the boat's prow now pointing to the sky, now showing us the way to the bottom of the sea; then waves breaking against the weather-counter, and deluging us with spray, all the time intent upon finding our cripple, and afraid, withal, to lose sight of our dead bird. Altogether, we had as lively a five minutes' search as any man need wish to have. To crown it all, a hailstorm burst upon us; and, upon my conscience, the hailstones were nearly as hard and as big as bullets, and they whacked us unmercifully on our ears, face, and hands, until we were made to smart all over, wherever our skin was exposed.

"Golly!" exclaimed my jolly tar, "one would think someone was firing big shot at us!"

Well, it really could hardly have been worse. Anyhow, it greatly increased our difficulties, for we could hardly see farther than five yards from the boat for a couple of minutes. However, in a momentary clearance, I caught sight of the blessed duck, and, quick as thought, I floored it.

"Got it?"

"Yes. It is dead this time."

"Good job, too," quoth the man, fervently.

"Amen to that," said I, laughing.

And we picked it up.

"Now, where is the other one?"

"Oh!" said he, "he has drifted down mid-channel. It won't be easy to find him."

"We will have a try, at any rate," I rejoined.

And we went.

The waves were so high and so "turmoily," that it was not easy to see anything about, but at last I perceived on the top of a wave a brown parcel tumbling about.

"I see it," cried I, "right ahead."

My man rowed me right up to it, and I laid hold of it as it floated past our port side.

"Now, home we go; I have had enough of this," I said.

"As it is," remarked he, "it is doubtful whether we shall manage to get back before dark."

However, we arrived just in time for the express, and I came back to town, rather pleased, after all, to be once more on the *plancher des vaches*.

A SECOND DAY'S WILDFOWLING ON THE ORWELL.

WELL, my previous trip having been so very moderately successful on account of the rough sea and weather I had experienced, I made up my mind to have another day on the Orwell, but to begin then at the estuary of the river; in one word, to start from Harwich, and come up as far as the spot where I had left off after shooting the two ducks. Accordingly, the next day but one saw me once more afloat, but this time I began operations almost before daylight. I had secured a boatman over night, and punctual to the minute, he came to fetch my gun and cartridges, and we walked to his craft, which was moored at the stone stairs opposite the hotel. A clear, bright, frosty morning it was, cold enough to make one's fingers tingle again, and one's ears feel rather *de trop*.

"Bound to get some birds to-day, I should think," I remarked.

"I will warrant you shall," said the fisherman, with a chuckle, and we got aboard.

No sooner was I comfortable than he cast her off, ran up the sail, and with a fair and stiffish breeze we threaded our course in the gloom through the shipping. How these men can make their way in complete darkness is a sort of mystery, but they do, and we found ourselves, after a twenty minutes' sail, just opposite the Nether Hall. The sea was running out, with the ebb-tide very strong, and the flats were once more reappearing. It was light enough then for good shooting, and the way the shore birds flew about us was a treat.

"Curr-liew! curr-liew!" by the long-billed birds; "Pee-wit! pee-wit!" by lapwings; plaintive "Peeho! peeho!" of waders; "Cwak! cwak!" of herons; and innumerable whistles were to be heard, and I had as nice shots for half an hour as I could desire to have.

First of all, at a long range I killed with No. 4 shot, from a 4-bore cartridge, three dunlins out of five, which were together flying towards the bank. My next shot floored four ring-plovers. The next two shots were misses. Then there was a lull, and sailing higher up, we were looking out for birds, when we heard several shots fired higher up the river, and a moment after a curlew passed us in full sail within fifty yards.

Boom! and he was cut down handsomely.

"There is another bird a-coming!" shouts my man.

I hurry up in my loading, but my fingers were so cold I could hardly get on. At last I have done.

"Whereabouts is the bird?" queried I then.

"I will sail her to him," replies the man; "it is a duck, I think, and he is on the sea, some way up. There he is!" calls he out a moment later.

I look up.

"That's not a duck," said I: "that's a grebe."

"So it is," says he; "but you are going to shoot it?"

"Rather."

Saying these words, I stoop in the bows, glancing along the gun-barrel, and when we get within eighty yards, as I perceive that the grebe is fidgety, and will very likely dive, as he raises his head to look at us, I pull, and—miss him, by all that's good! The boat had lurched just in the nick of time, and the shot was pitched right under the bird. He, of course, dived at once, and I reloaded in silence.

"There he goes!" said my man presently, looking astern.

"Let us go back to him," urged I.

"Better sail away, and round again," represented he.

"Please yourself, but give me another chance at the grebe."

We were about a quarter of an hour at this business, but eventually I got the grebe. We then went to the northern shore, and seeing about a dozen curlews together, we put down mast and sail and rowed up to them. When we were about half-way I stood up in the boat, and there were the birds feeding away. On seeing my head, one called and all jumped up; but the terrible load came among them, and two of them were literally smashed.

It was then getting about one P.M. We had a snack whilst in the creek, then rowed out, and I shot, on our way back, a diver in mid-stream and a heron on a mud bank, and thus ended my trip to the Orwell—total for the two days' sport, nineteen birds, viz. three dunlins, eight ring-plovers, three curlews, two ducks, one heron, one grebe, and one diver.

There were loads of birds about, and several boats were in chase, among which a ten-ton cutter rather distinguished itself by firing a stanchion gun in such a manner that its shot flew around us, and we picked up a shot in the boat. Had the weather kept at all severe, good bags would have been the rule, but at the time of writing this the weather was quite mild—disgustingly so, in fact. However, let us hope for the best, and I trust we will soon have snow and frost to our heart's content, so that the wildfowl guns may have fair sport. The papers said that the Baltic harbours were blocked with ice. Could not they spare us a little of that precious commodity? I, for one, wish they would.

The illustration, entitled "Wildfowling on the Orwell," which appeared in *The Country*, from a rough sketch of mine, shows how the sport is carried on in the estuaries when the flocks, in severe weather, turn up. With a stout and stiff dinghy, a pretty bold crew of sportsmen (not averse to "roughing" it), and a fairly powerful swivel-gun, excellent execution can be done among the fowl; and the sport, when thus carried on, is far more sociable and pleasurable than punting. I have spent many very happy days thus, with companions endowed with the same sporting spirit, and I can safely say that no sport can beat wildfowling, when enjoyed in that style, for fun, good-fellowship, and sterlingly genuine amusement.

The cripple chase which follows the firing of the big gun is invariably a most exciting piece of business. On the day to which the illustration refers, in January, 1870, I had fired the stanchion with such success that we picked up altogether nineteen or twenty birds, seven or eight of which were but very slightly crippled, and consequently led us a perfect dance, all the more enjoyable, of course, as snow was falling the whole day, so persistently that we could hardly see to shape our course. However, that is just the sort of weather for sport, and should we get something like it this winter, I warrant the stanchion men would reap a good harvest at the mouths of the Crouch, the Blackwater, the Orwell, and the Deben, on the east coast, and at Chichester and Poole Harbour on the south coast.

SEA-FISHING TRIPS.

SEA-FISHING TRIPS.

FILEY BRIGG.

FILEY BRIGG (or bridge) is simply a belt of rocks extending no inconsiderable distance to sea, and forming a capital stand for shore-hookers, who, taking their station there, can fish in all sorts of weather, changing side with the wind. The Brigg is about a mile north of Filey, and the walk there over the sands is simply charming, the more so as many people usually take up their winter residence at Filey, and when the sun shines the sands are well tenanted by visitors, who pick up shells, read novels, and flirt, like the vast majority of seaside visitors.

There are always a few enthusiastic sea-fishermen at Filey, and these are to be seen every morning wending their way to the Brigg. They lunch there, and generally come back in company.

The little town is wonderfully neat and clean. It is perched up on a not very high cliff, and some pretty houses facing the sea afford a lively prospect of the German Ocean. The terms are, I am told, for a continued residence, remarkably cheap—a couple of sovereigns a week keeping the sportsman in thorough comfort; and I should certainly recommend the place to anyone in search of a healthy, pleasant, and interesting spot, where sport, in the hooking line, without having to go to sea, is considered a *sine quâ non*. Many seaports have piers from which one may angle, but the traffic is generally troublesome, and the timbers of the piers have a knack of getting in the way of the hooks.

At Filey there is absolutely no traffic about the Brigg, for all boats take care to give it a wide berth on account of the sunken rocks which abound in its neighbourhood. The only trouble to contend against is with those same sunken rocks, for bringing to hand a loaded line over a rocky bottom is far from a joke. It requires practice and a good stout rod, and I have seen many fishers lose half-a-dozen hooks running at the Brigg, precisely because they were lacking in practised tact and proper equipment. A stout and moderately long rod, with but little "spring," is, I have found, the best tool to undertake this affair with. Having baited your hooks, spread the lead and hooks on a clean piece of rock, let out some of your line handy, as many yards as you fancy you will need, and coil it backwards, so that it will go with a run when shying your lead. Then bring up the end of the line along your rod, so as to have your weight about six feet from the top of the rod, tighten the line along the rod, and hold the line with your right hand; then lift up rod and line, swing the lead backwards, shy it forwards, and rather high, so as to command a good swing, and let go the string. The line will jump through the top ring like an arrow, and you will thus secure an excellent "throw," unless your line gets entangled and reaches the top ring in a "lump," when the weight of the lead, multiplied by the square of its impetus, produces such a strain that you hear a plain "snap," and lo! hooks and lead are gone, truly, many yards to sea; but your "connecting link" is rather disconnected. Even supposing you have succeeded in producing a good "throw," you have only done as yet the easiest part of the affair. Bringing up your line to hand again without damage is *the* difficulty. It is tantalising when you have hooked a fish to find that, as you are bringing it up, a great long arm of seaweed deliberately uncoils itself out of its dark cavern under the rocks, then with a dash of the tide it springs forth like a thing of life, and entwines itself, in hideous confusion, with line, hooks, lead, and fish. Then it is a simple case of pull devil, pull baker, and ten to one that the weeds eventually beat the fisherman.

There are boats at Filey, but there is no pier, and that precluded my going straight to Filey, as, in the event of there having been anything of a sea on, the chances would have been a hundred to one that no boatman would have been willing to launch his craft from the sands. As to fishing from the Brigg itself, I have done a great deal of it already, and would rather be at sea. I therefore arranged to go to Scarborough, where a friend of mine resides, and he very kindly undertook to secure a nice craft for our outing. We were five altogether—two boatmen to manage the craft, my friend, with a friend of his, and myself. We had brought our guns with us, on the off-chance of meeting with some of the Flamborough birds about, as we did not expect any ducks or widgeons, and in this surmise we were quite correct.

By-the-way, it may not be out of place for me to point

out to enthusiastic wildfowl-shooters that an alteration has again taken place as regards the dates of the close season for shooting wildfowl, and as a good deal of uncertainty exists as to what is "wildfowl," and what is a "sea-bird," it will be well for shooters to study the following lists, and to refer to them, if need ever be, before pulling trigger, as the penalties have been increased. Thus, after the 15th . . . one may shoot an oyster-catcher, but curlews then will be sacred, &c. &c. . . . Would not it be better to make a close season for all birds, beginning and ending, for all, on the same date? Between the 15th of February and the 10th of July, in most places, under the penalty of such a sum of money, not exceeding one pound, as the justices or sheriff shall seem meet, together with the costs of the conviction, the following "wildfowl" must not be shot :—the different species of avocet, curlew, dotterel, dunbird, dunlin, godwit, greenshank, lapwing, mallard, oxbird, peewit, phalarope, plover, plover's-page, pochard, purre, redshank, reeve or ruff, sanderling, sandpiper, sea-lark, shoveller, snipe, spoonbill, stint, stone curlew, stone-hatch, summer-snipe, teal, thick-knee, whaup, whimbrel, widgeon, wild duck, wild goose, and woodcock. For "sea-birds," the close season is still between the 1st of April and the 1st of August. "Sea-birds," according to the Act, are "the different species of auk, bonxie, Cornish coulterneb, diver, eider-duck, fulmar, gannet, grebe, chough, guillemot, gull, kittiwake, loon, marrot, merganser, murre, oyster-catcher, petrel, puffin, razor-bill, scout, seamew, sea parrot, sea swallow, shearwater, shelldrake, skua, smew, solan goose, tarrock, tern, tystey, and willock." This being so, it will behove sea-shooters to be careful in the handling of their firearms, and short-sighted men, or men with limited ornithological knowledge, had better abstain altogether.

The staple baits for sea-fishing on the Yorkshire coast consist of mussels, herring-roe or milt, and lugworms. The latter are always somewhat limited in quantity, though I fail to see why, as the muddy sands at low tide ought to give a pretty fair harvest of lugs to a diligent investigator. But the maritime population—at least the juvenile part of it—are chary of attending to it, and mussels being procurable in boatsful, the fishermen are content with that.

As regards the herring-milt, it is not always procurable, as it has to undergo a certain preparation; and those old "salts" who have a provision thereof, do not care about parting with it, because, when properly stiff and fair, it is one of the best killing baits on the coast.

Lugs come, I believe, next in attractiveness. Mussels are awkward things to fix on one's hooks, and it is positively laborious to keep three hooks tolerably well supplied. Some men twine a little worsted round the mussel, so as to secure it on the hook, but it is awkward and troublesome. Personally, I prefer lugs to all baits.

Whilst on our way due south towards Filey, we prepared our lines, and I found that my two companions, being Scarborough men, were thoroughly versed in the pursuit we were engaged upon. It appeared that they frequently went out in boats, or when the weather was bad they fished from the piers at Scarborough, so that as a rule they had two or three days a week at that game, and this explained the wonderful quickness of touch which subsequently distinguished all their operations. To disentangle a lot of lines which seemed hopelessly mixed together was, for them, a labour of love, and baiting was performed in a sort of legerdemain fashion, as they rolled a mussel with wool on three hooks in a twinkling, fishing meanwhile with the other hand; in fact, they were better hands at that game than many a professional.

The rocks in a portion of the high cliffs which extend between Filey Brigg and Scarborough overhang each other in marvellous style, and carry on that fashion to the very bottom of the sea, so that when the day is clear and the sea smooth, by peering over the gun'ale of a boat, one may see at great depths a lot of deep, dark caverns, whose black mouths are lined with weeds. From these mouths issue now and again monstrous fish of all sizes, forms, and colours.

On the day of our excursion the sea was as quiet as a mill-pond in the morning, so that we took matters very coolly, rowing close in shore, frequently going in to inspect the old caves, and trying all sorts of baits in a charmingly-desultory fashion. There we were, bobbing quietly to the swell of the ocean, with a bright sun overhead, green and white and brown cliffs and rocks in front of us, and a smooth and placid sea gently lapping against the hard rocks, and the sport, meanwhile, was superb. Whilst two of us were occupied with our deep lines, my friend with his stiff rod and a spinner, supplemented by a strip of skin below it, was "trailing" all round the boat.

Our men were a pleasant couple, and gave us no trouble. As soon as we were at anchor, they laid themselves down in the bows, pulled their tarpaulins over their legs, lit their pipes, looked at us, and were seemingly thoroughly happy.

The first place we stopped at was just underneath the high cliff, and in front of us was a large cave, into which we could have taken the boat had we chosen to do so, but the men did not seem to see it. We had, however, dropped our moorings within forty yards of the cave, and it was most interesting to see the denizens of the deep in their incursions and excursions to and fro.

First came a monstrous cod, with great goggle eyes. He sailed solemnly round a rock, where seaweeds brushed his back and his stomach as he passed through them, and he seemed to like the process. He sniffed at my bait, passed by, went round astern, and I lost sight of him. I turned my head back, having announced the cod's visit to my neighbour, and the latter was just saying, "I see him! Here he comes! Wonder if he will take my bait;" when, simultaneously, we both jumped up.

"I have got him!" he said; and "I have got two!" exclaimed I; and we hauled away joyfully. Mine were about eighteen inches long, and their beards were of decent length, but my friend's catch was quite venerable in comparison to mine, and he weighed seven or eight pounds for certain.

Now our men had been told that, barring a few fish which we would keep for ourselves, if we thought fit, the rest of our catches would be theirs, and accordingly the sight of the cod put them on their thoroughly pleasant behaviour. They came forward to unhook our fish, and instead of remaining lazily smoking in the bows, they spontaneously commenced preparing our bait, unhooking our fish, and making themselves generally useful. This was as it should be, but it is really rare to meet with very attentive boatmen, and the only sure way of enlisting their sympathies is to give them a pecuniary interest in your proceedings. As a rule this will be found a very powerful and inducing argument.

When we had collared our codlings, we remained on watch, and other cods made their appearance, together with some lively pollack and some whacking billet. One of them caused quite a sensation. He took the spinner, and being evidently bent on a voyage of discovery with it, darted into some crevices in the rocks, and disappeared, our companion's rod bobbing about like a broomstick, with about as much spring withal. He held on tightly, but the fish was bent on effecting a separation, and between the two we were wonderfully annoyed, as in a moment two of the three lines out were in an almost hopeless tangle, and there was every likelihood of the third line also coming in for a share of the confusion. I saw the fish several times in his perambulations.

For some reason, best known to himself, he had evidently taken hold of the lower hook, so that the spinner most ludicrously stuck at the side of his mouth close to his left eye. I believe the fish was lost through the lines getting foul of each other. When brought up they were discovered to be sadly knotted and twisted, but they were in the hands of experts, and before long both were again clear and at work, and the pollack soon showed grand sport with the spinner.

It requires considerable knack and skill to manage a spinner from a stationary boat at sea. Of course the boat, though moored, is always labouring under the swell of the sea, and to stand up in such a craft and handle the rod so as to make the spinner travel from bow to stern and back again, on either side, without too much or too little speed, and to strike just at the right time requires much practice. It was certainly sport under great difficulties to bring the fish up, when they were heavy, before they had time to get themselves through a maze of weeds and the line in a mess with the tough creeping things which there covered the rocks at the bottom of the sea, waving about with the tide's motions like a wheat-field in harvest time under the breath of a strong wind.

We remained at the same spot as long as fish came to meet our baits there, *i.e.* some two hours, when, unaccountably, they deserted the spot, and we could only catch small fish. These were too small to induce us to remain any longer, and accordingly we told our men to prepare for departure, and in two or three minutes we were off. By that time, about noon, there were some half-dozen boats out also fishing, and noticing that they made it a point to try the open sea, we followed suit, and all I can say is that had we been half-a-dozen hookers instead of only three, I believe we should have found fish enough to tax the energies of all. Whiting and pouting abounded, and bit freely, frequently three fish coming up at one haul. Some were not heavy enough to suit us, and we returned them as soon as freed. Mussel bait is rather disgusting to handle, as it messes one's hands dreadfully, so that these desperate feeders were rather annoying in their obstinate attentions, but soon a lot of large fish scattered the youngsters like chaff before a hurricane. I saw it all. There were about twenty small fish in a lump round my line, nibbling away, and darting together occasionally at some loose morsel of bait, when suddenly there sailed up with solemn gravity a school of codlings, headed by a veteran, and flanked by two or three red gurnards of imposing size, and lo! the small fry darted hither and thither in terrible fright, and in a twinkling not one remained. Not for long, however, for they soon recovered from their panic, and mingled afterwards pretty fearlessly with the throng, until two or three sharky-looking dog-fish, with evil eyes and hungry jaws, turned up in their midst, when large and small fish skedaddled with all speed; but one or two of the rearmost, I think, were captured, and an unfortunate one which was on my companion's line was actually seized and cut in two by one of the voracious rascals.

After that, when peering into the sea, it appeared, as far as the eye could reach, a perfect wilderness; but on looking carefully along the bottom, we could perceive the dark green backs of the "sharks," steadily lying in wait among the rocks, like bandits in the passes of a mountain. There being nothing to be done until they were either caught or replete with food, we threw some half-dozen whiting overboard, and the wrangling and fierce tearing which took place reminded me very much of two or three sharp terriers worrying rats. We tried to hook them, but did not succeed, and when duly satisfied with their meal they left us, and the other fish came back.

We changed our place soon afterwards, and stood about a mile to sea, just in front of the Brigg, whereon, we could perceive, were two or three hookers hard at work. We were in a capital place, and with only one more hour to spare, we used the remainder of our bait freely, and were rewarded with excellent sport. I very much regretted having no long line with us (and no time to set it, if we had had one), on account of the tantalising sight of four professional fishermen close to us, who were lifting their long lines and filled their boat with fish. Still we got on exceedingly well, and being in a deep part, our fish were heavier, as a rule, than the general run of those we had caught previously. We had whiting by the score, about half-a-dozen congers, more or less (they were so mixed up we could not tell which from which), half a score of billet and coal-pollack, a dozen good-sized codlings, nine or ten skate, over ten large-sized gray and red gurnards, and the usual riff-raff sure to be caught anywhere when sea-fishing.

Now if any hooker should try Filey as a sea-fishing station I think he will like it. It is not a poor little fishing village, in an out-of-the-way place, and totally uncome-at-able like most fishing villages. It is a rising little town, frequented by nice people, with fair shops, good lodgings and hotels, a railway station of some pretensions, plenty of good sands, good cliffs, nice drives, and nice walks, with the certainty of good sport at most times, either from the Brigg or from boats, which are obtainable at the shortest notice in fine weather.

SCARBOROUGH AND WHITBY.

OF course, after our trip to Filey, I had resolved upon giving Scarborough a good trial before turning my face towards town, but I scarcely could see my way to an inspection of the Whitby fishing-grounds, as time was passing, and I knew the journey from Scarborough to Whitby by train to be one of unconscionable length.

I had had only three days originally at my disposal. One I had spent fishing at Filey; the second was pretty far advanced when we awoke from our slumbers the morning after the trip I last narrated; but still we had enough time left to see, during the remainder of the day, what sport Scarborough could offer us, and this left only the third day to devote to Whitby. My friend solved the difficulty in the following manner: "We are only twenty miles or so," said he, "from Whitby. What is to prevent us from going out fishing now, until two or three P.M., and then set sail for Whitby? We shall get there by nine or ten this evening, and to-morrow can be devoted to fishing in the Roads. Then we can either sail back here, or you may take your train back to London from Whitby, direct."

As regards Scarborough, to the man who delights in trying his hand in the sea-fishing line, the harbour offers plenty of chances, for, from whichever way the wind blows, from three-quarter flow to half-ebb he can always indulge in the pursuit, and may fish either from the piers, or from some of the smacks at their moorings, or he may hire a boat for his own fishing at very moderate terms, especially if he is a permanent customer to the boatman. I remember very well having a boat offered me at Scarborough, if regularly taken, at the rate of thirty shillings, or two pounds, a month.

Now admitting the first amount, for the sake of argument, it will be seen that the average rate was simply a little over one shilling a day, calculating at six days' outing every week. This offer, however, was made some time since, and I should not wonder if the terms have risen with everything else; but even if a man pays two pounds a month for the use of a boat he cannot grumble, and the owner of the boat must be pleased with his bargain.

As regards fishing in Scarborough harbour itself, this is only available at such times as already stated, because at low tide the harbour is dry, or nearly so. But when the tide is rising, anyone taking his stand on the piers is pretty sure to fill his creel, if not with dabs and plaice, then with codlings, parrs, small gurnards, and codfish, and in the rocks he will find a few congers, together with not a few crabs, anemones, and other "nuisances." It is, however, rather rare to see anything weighty caught in that style, and one stands a much better chance by getting on board a smack or a brig and fishing from the deck. Leave is always granted quite readily by the skippers, who seemingly delight in having land-lubbers aboard.

I remember once seeing about a dozen hookers at work

on board a coal brig in the harbour, and the crew and captain were lying down on deck, amongst the creels and spare lines, smoking their pipes and enjoying the fun. As regards fishing from the piers, a stranger would be surprised to see the immense number of men and lads who resort to it. I noted down, one day, fifteen hookers on the piers, and "would anyone be surprised to hear" that a sweep was the very next neighbour to a lord? The bait dealers, fishermen themselves, drive a roaring trade in Scarborough, and it is not uncommon to see half-a-dozen hookers, whose bait is scarce, running eagerly from cottage to cottage, inquiring about the precious commodity.

Moreover, such is the love of sea-fishing with the population in general, that near the piers I know several men who keep a regular assortment of tackle of all sorts ready to let out.

Suppose half-a-dozen men are hooking, and about forty or fifty idlers are looking on; presently one of the hookers will bring to book a whacking pollack, conger, or codling. Thereupon a stampede takes place amongst the lookers-on. In two minutes they are rigged out, fully accoutred, and back to the pier like an invading army. In five more minutes every point of vantage is seized upon, and as the Scarborough men are doughty fishermen, the finny tribe have to look very sharp to avoid being caught. Those who are fond of large fish will have to go to sea. It is rare that anything above two or three pounds is caught from the piers, except when a strong wind blows from shore.

For general good sport, nothing can beat the belt of rocks some two or three miles away to sea, and nearly opposite the town.

I would advise anybody intending to try that place not to lose time when going there, but trail all the way, when he will find excellent fun with parrs, if he catches nothing heavier. On our excursion we acted up to that dodge. I got a mackerel line, to which I appended, below the boat-shaped lead, a long flight of flies, followed by the usual spinner, thinking that perhaps it would not be a bad plan to allow it to remain, and as soon as we were fairly under weigh I dropped it astern, gently towing it up and down, without any too sudden motion. I got a bite almost immediately, then, soon after, two or three wriggles testified that the flies were killing, and I got three parrs in, half-pounders.

Going along the pier easily, my friend, who had taken his turn at the line, caught two and four more, respectively in two casts, and when we cleared the harbour a great fish took the hook, smashed the line, and went away, carrying all the flies with him. It must have been a pollack of good weight. Precisely at the same moment a pier angler was hauling up two rattling good fish of the same species. Our flies being gone, one of us set about refixing a flight of them, and, meanwhile, we had time to look about us.

In the midst of our contemplation of the beauties of Scarborough, two or three companies of widgeon passed us going south. Of course, they were then sacred in the British kingdom, and, therefore, even if we had had our guns, we could not have shot them with impunity; but this led us to talk about the Wildfowl Act, and it strikes me as being rather odd that most of the British shores should from the 15th . . . protect birds, which, on some parts of the Continent, may be shot all the year round. Would it not have been better to secure a uniform date of protection from every other European country? What is the use of protecting anything which others, within twenty miles or so of England, may kill with impunity?

Whilst discussing this matter, we had been making good way. Our men had set the sail, and we were spinning along in fine style, so that within a little over half an hour we reached our fishing-ground that was to be. Our men took their bearings, down came the sail, and down went our moorings. We cleared the stern-seats, and had our work cut out to do so, because we had brought extra greatcoats, rugs, and provisions, so that the craft was rather full.

My portmanteau was singularly in the way; I intended taking a night train from Whitby, and of course had had to bring my luggage with us. However, a happy thought struck me, and we transformed the portmanteau into a seat, and it had a few fish scales stuck about ere we had done, so that it looked pretty much like a fish salesman's property when I went on my railway journey.

We were about two hours fishing. Taught by experience, we only used very stout gear, with wire-plaited snoodings, and did not lose a single line, although we had some very heavy fish. We did not catch so many as at Filey, but, considering the short time we were at it, our average was quite as fair. The wind then shifted south, and was fair for our journey. Still, as we had a good distance to cover, it was deemed advisable to set about it as early as possible, in case the weather should have turned uncomfortable, and accordingly at half-past two P.M. we cleared the seats, and away we went full sail for Whitby. One of our companions whiffed part of the way, with three fair pollack as a result. The sail was very pleasurable at first, as we kept within a mile of the shore, and could see the villages along the coast, without needing the use of the glass.

Somehow, when it became dark we became dull, conversation dropped, and we smoked our pipes in silence. Had we had a cabin to retire to, it would have been all right; but as it was, having no protection against the night air and the cold wind, no wonder a "wet blanket" was spread over our feelings. However, I groped in the dark, and by the light of a fusee, I fished out a bottle of sherry from the hamper. We could not find the corkscrew, so I knocked off the neck of the bottle, and we had a drain all round in a beer glass. Then the men grew lively, and my companions more chatty, and we yarned away the time pleasantly enough.

At half-past seven we passed Robin Hood's Bay, and on turning the Point the Whitby Lighthouse hove in sight, and our spirits rose. The wind held on, we took the sweeps by turns, and at half-past nine were entering the harbour in company with half-a-dozen professional hookers' boats. We ran up the stairs, and were thankful to get our legs "under the mahogany" without delay.

At our hotel we found two gentlemen who had been hooking all day in the Roads, and their narrative of the sport they had met there made us wish the night over.

The morning was not bright, but there was little or no wind. I was surprised at not seeing any more boats out (I mean with amateurs), because I know that several parties make it their business to let boats on hire in the harbour; but my friend suggested that the afternoon, when fine, is usually the time chosen by visitors for their sea-fishing trips, and so it turned out to be, for when we came back we saw about half-a-dozen out.

I cannot say that for sea-fishing proper these rowing boats are well adapted; they are, to my fancy, too light, and roll about so that it makes the hookers very speedily uncomfortable, unless they happen to be thoroughly inured to the sea.

I remember once being in one of these boats, and nearly upsetting it when bringing up a fish; in fact, the gun'ale was within a quarter of an inch of getting under. I advise amateurs not to put up with such nutshells; a stiff, heavy boat is the thing.

Just before we reached our station we had a most extraordinary incident. I was leisurely whiffing with two or three flies and a silver spinner, when, turning astern, I saw that, owing to a sudden gust of wind which had filled our sail and made the boat spin along and "tell tales," my bait had come up and was within half a foot of the surface of the sea. "I ought to put a heavier weight for this speed," I was arguing within myself, when suddenly there appeared close to my spinner a tremendous dogfish, about a yard long. Of course I knew he was bent on having a go at my bright spinner, but I knew that my spinning line (let alone the gut trace) would never hold such a fellow as that a second, so I hauled up the line suddenly just when he was striking, and he missed, of course; and to save the line I hurriedly hauled it along, intending to get it aboard, and substitute for it another. But the brute was not to be denied, and made such a well-timed and well-directed rush that in an instant I had a bare bit of line in my hand. "You beast!" I exclaimed involuntarily, "I will make you pay for this, or my name is not—'Wildfowler.'"

We upset my creel to find out a wire line, and having got it, down we got the sail. The line I used was one of my own making, and should any fisherman wish to have one of the same thoroughly teeth-proof qualities, the following is my manner of making it:

Take a deal board, two feet long and two inches thick. Bore through it with a gimlet two holes about a foot apart. If the gimlet be of the diameter of an ordinary pencil, so much the better. In these two holes, then, insert two whole pencils, and indent them (about two inches from the board) with a superficial cut. Turn these cuts away from each other, and draw some fine copper wire from each to each as many times as you may think may be needed for the strength required. Half-a-dozen turns each way generally satisfy me. When you have done so, cut the wire, join the two ends, and twist them together; then remove the two pencils bodily, and twist them contrariwise. This will twist the wire, and make of it a sort of copper cord which will defy anything but a crocodile's teeth, and that is the sort of snooding I generally use for large congers and dog-fish. Of course, where the two pencils have held the snooding, two loops necessarily exist. To one of these loops secure the hook, and, to the other, fix a swivel through which to connect the snooding with the main line. With that sort of line one is safe, as nothing short of a shark can possibly break it through.

It was with a line of that sort that I set about trying for the thief who had just run away with my spinner. I baited with one of our small pollack, and let go the half-pound weight. When it reached the bottom I gradually brought it up, just as I had done originally with the first line; but nothing came of these tactics.

"You pricked him with the spinner," said one of my companions, "and he is shy now."

"I suppose he is," I rejoined, and began to feel rather doubtful of success; but suddenly the line slid through my hand, and "ran" on the gun'ale. "I have got him!" I called out, and safe enough I had; but the way he kicked, plunged, and dived was most extraordinary. He literally moved the boat in his frantic efforts, but it was no use. I only gave him line when I could not hold him tight, and I brought him up slowly but surely within the reach of the gaff, when one of the men got him at the neck, and jerked him on to the floor.

He was quite a yard long, and was the biggest I had caught for some years. The wire snooding was quite marked by his teeth, and—hurrah! the silver spinner was in him, and we got it back, after all. We should never have thought of looking for the spinner in his gullet, had not one of the flies been still sticking out of his jaws.

When we had despatched him, we set about hooking in earnest, and as we had the whole day before us, lots of bait, good company, plenty of refreshments and tobacco, and nothing that I am aware of on our consciences, everything tended to make of ours a jolly trip.

There were at least ten boats about us, two of which had amateurs on board, and one of these turned out to be our hotel companion of the previous night.

"There is," said he, in the course of conversation, when he had drawn near to exchange news, "a sporting writer who signs himself 'Wildfowler,' who goes about sea-fishing, and tells his adventures in *Bell's Life*. I wonder he does not come here. Why, I am now tired of bringing up my fish, and if he knew what sport is to be had here what an article he would make of it!"

At this my friends burst out laughing, and I then told him that I was the "Wildfowler" mentioned, and received a hearty greeting from him.

We fished on within four or five yards of each other, and it was a pleasant way of pursuing the sport. Our new acquaintance was an expert, and an enthusiastic sea fisherman, and he declared that sea-fishing was better than even fly-fishing! Rank heresy, no doubt, in many men's estimation.

He fully endorsed my opinions about ordinary tackle, as expressed in one of my papers, and showed me some hooks which he had recently purchased, which were so straight as to make them anything but killing.

"I should bend them," I suggested.

"How?" inquired he.

"Why, with pliers," I rejoined. "I have got a pair here. Shall I lend them to you?"

He agreed to try, and declared his hooks, when bent, to be all right. There are many hooks with the same defect, which can be altered, but small ones, highly tempered, do not brook any liberties, and break like glass, unless they are first heated, then bent to the required shape, and then re-tempered. All this is troublesome, and the makers ought to turn out hooks with irreproachable curves, even if they were to charge a little more for them. Of course, in first-rate shops one gets first-rate articles; but then these shops are not always handy, and what is a sea fisherman to do when he finds himself in an out-of-the-way village?

We found our fish to be similar to those we had caught at Filey, viz. codlings, congers, skate, gurnards, pouting, coalfish, &c., and we took so many that our two men could not land the whole at Whitby under two journeys each, up and down the harbour stairs.

So much for the sport to be had there. As regards accommodation, bait, boats, and boatmen, no one need be under any apprehension who wishes to make Whitby his headquarters for sea-fishing. It is one of the best-supplied stations on the coast, and anybody trying the sport there is sure to get his fill of it.

OFF THE NORTH FORELAND AND OFF THE BLACK ROCK.

YACHTSMEN are like the scene-shifters of theatres in one respect, viz. they see at times their sundry stages in their utter nakedness. Such was my reflection when, from the deck of our ten-tonner, I looked at the town of Ramsgate, yet wrapped up in its slumbers. There it was, all dark and gloomy; its street lamps flared quite yellow, its streets were deserted, save by hungry cats and dogs, its windows were carefully blinded. From the shipping came no sound, and but for the everlasting murmuring sea, one might have been excused for imagining himself in a dream.

The morning was cold and bracing, for a wonder. After our late downpour, it was quite a change to see a clear sky, and I felt hopeful once more. We began getting the sheets loose without loss of time, and the creaking of our windlass brought up two or three heads on the decks of our neighbours.

"Going off?" inquired an acquaintance.

"Yes, fishing," was our reply.

"Wish you luck," and with a glance at the sky the speaker returned to his bunk, vowing mentally, no doubt, that we must have been mad to slip our moorings so early.

There was a nice breeze blowing straight away, and, with a slack mainsail, still further extended over our port side by means of a long sweep lashed to the counter, we made excellent way. I had heard that excellent sport was to be had off the North Foreland and along the Channel, and having provided ourselves with a good deal of bait, there was every likelihood that we should spend a pleasant day at sea, if the weather remained as it was.

When we were about four miles from the lightship we saw a rather curious sight. There was a yacht going, to all appearance, the same road as ourselves, and, in fact, our owner had made up his mind to try and catch her, when he suddenly observed that she was altering her course. We took up our glasses, and saw three fellows crouching forward with guns; and presently, when they had been on their new course for about a quarter of a mile, they jumped up and fired. Then we saw about fifteen birds flying away, and two of the men got into the dinghy, evidently to pick up those that had been shot. This delayed their yacht, and we soon came up to them, just when the shooters were boarding her again, and they had three widgeons.

In astonishment I said to them: "What about the Act?" for the season was closed.

"The Act be blowed!" said one; "those who made it don't know what is what! Why, I warrant if we showed them these widgeons, and swore they were not 'wild-fowl,' but 'sea-birds,' they would not know any better. These will go into the pot, at any rate."

"We will lay an information against you," I said laughing.

"All right," they returned; "you had better come aboard and have your share of them. In that way you will be sure they are widgeons!"

And with that we parted, they heading south, probably in search of other "sea-birds" of the same species.

"Now," said my friend, "where shall we anchor?"

"Let us try the lead," suggested he, "and when we find a good depth, stay there."

The man from the stern quietly heaved the lead until he announced eight fathoms, when we became all attention, and leaving our cards on the table (we were having a game at *écarté*), went on deck to see where we were. The sight was a very strange one. There was not a single sail for many miles, but in the distance were innumerable craft crawling along. The wind had died out, and had it not been for the tide swelling up under the yacht, we should have been stationary. The sea was very smooth notwithstanding, the long tide-waves reaching to an enormous breadth before breaking, the sun was hidden behind some clouds, and I thought as the depth pretty well suited us, and we might not for hours get a breeze, that we had better stop where we were; so giving the word, we rattled the anchor overboard, and soon came to a decided full stop, when we prepared our gear, without, however, any intention of using it until breakfast was over.

Meanwhile all sail was taken in, everything made snug, and then the men went below to lay the cloth. We had a good sound meal, and a couple of glasses of sherry over it; then we lit our pipes, and went to take our respective stations, I on the port side, and my friend on the starboard, both enjoying the sea air and the motion of the sea to the utmost.

When I first brought up my line, with a couple of dabs on, I asked: "Was that a drop of rain that fell on my nose just now?"

Quoth my friend: "I have had one too; I thought at first you had splashed me."

Then we looked around, and saw that the sea was getting quite steady and flat, and a good many extending circles very soon rippled its surface, breaking it into a dull, leady-like sheet.

"Tom, bring the sou'-westers and oilskin. Look sharp!"

"Ay, ay, sir."

And the man came out of the cabin presently with a lot of waterproof contrivances.

Now when a man is clad in yellow stiff breeches, and an equally yellow and, if anything, a stiffer over-all, capped with another yellow contrivance, with a flap behind, that extends to the middle of his back (more or less), with the grace and elegance of goods of Hottentot manufacture, he does not look fashionable, and Regent Street tailors would unanimously disclaim having had any hand in his outfit. Yet it is very handy, though not comely or comfortable, and we did not even laugh when we looked at each other, and found ourselves transformed into something very like two tremendously large and yellow beetles. Then, with a steady rain coming down upon us, we pursued our sport.

We had been fishing about half an hour when my friend, wanting to go in the cabin for a "mixture," relinquished his line to his man, who presently brought up his line, looked over the side, and said he had a conger.

"No congers here," I said.

"Well, an eel, then."

"Very doubtful," I rejoined.

"Then," he said, "what in the name of all that is guid is that?"

And he flung on deck a garfish—a monster, in superb condition.

I was rather surprised. How the fish had managed to hook himself on the single hook passed my comprehension, for the inside of their mouth (I ought rather to say beak) is nearly as hard as London pavement, and a fish of that sort must be indeed intent upon committing suicide to fiddle about a hook a sufficiently long time to get it inserted at last into one or other of his jaws.

"I know what it be now," quoth the sailor; "them fish is what they call snipe-fish, ain't they, sir?"

"Well, perhaps; but they have so many names that really I can't tell. Some call them long-noses, others long-snouts, some snipe-bills, and others large sand-eels. The real name, however, is garfish."

My friend then came up and resumed his station, bringing soon after two or three more of these queer fish. Strange to say, I did not catch a single one. The moment I feel the slightest bite up I jerk the line, and, of course, for such fish that system won't do, as it merely scratches them, and does not prick them at all. They ought to be allowed ample time to gorge, and, moreover, a mackerel treble hook would be far more certain in its action with them, because whichever way the garfish got the bait in, there would be sure to be at least one hook out of the three that would secure him. But the fact of the matter was, I was well aware of their tactics, and did not wish to catch them. I don't think them nice eating, by any means, whereas dabs and gurnards are very excellent.

We did not see a single mackerel, but we had a rare lot of gurnards (red ones) and dabs. I have rarely seen the latter so numerous. We continually got them up, by twos and threes, and at times, both of us having our lines on deck together, we had as many as five and six fish splashing about. The man had placed a tub close by for us to put our fish in as soon as unhooked, and had very sensibly poured into it a pailful or two of sea-water, so as to keep the fish alive and in good trim until such time as they would be required for the table; but we caught them at such a rate that within two hours the tub was so full of fish that the water only superficially covered the lot, and whenever a newcomer was added to the tribe, not only this newcomer himself, but all the others, which he disturbed by his arrival, set about flapping energetically, and the effect thereof was as good a sea-water shower-bath over our oilskins as any man need wish to have. We therefore advised our "canny" man of the north to return to the sea those of our fish that were not sufficiently large to warrant their being detained. He, however, contented himself with picking them out and placing them in a separate pail, remarking that it would not do to pitch them back, "because they would bite again, and he would look a fool putting back into the sea the same fish over and over again."

Towards two o'clock the rain ceased, the sky cleared, and the wind got up. We then discussed the question of our return journey. I felt in the humour for a long night sail, especially as the weather had turned so bright; so it was agreed that we should make a night of it on the green sea. We remained at our new station until about half-past six, when the shades of evening began spreading themselves over the sea.

With the first twinkling of the lights ashore the Goodwin North Sands light-vessel began to show his three-lights; the North Foreland lighthouse on our port side lighted up also; and several steamers in sight, going up and down, showed their red and green and white lights. Our men got ours in order too; then we wound up our tackle, put aside the tub of sizeable fish, pitched astern the others, emptied ditto our bait cans, got up our anchor, ran up the jib, foresail, and mainsail, and under a steady breeze we rounded into the Channel homeward bound. Twenty minutes later we were passing Margate, and keeping well within the cliff banks end we spun along and soon cleared into the Horse Channel. All was plain sailing then for a couple of hours. We passed Herne Bay and Whitstable, and entered the mouth proper of old Father Thames.

With the increasing darkness the wind increased also, but the moon eventually made its appearance, and this enlivened our excursion very considerably. Time flew by so quickly that I was surprised when we were passing Sheerness to find that it was two A.M. Then I turned in for four hours, and when I turned up again we were at Coal House Point, from whence I took charge of the boat, and at ten o'clock we were at Erith, and the cable rattled down for good, and thus ended our sea-fishing excursion to the North Foreland.

We had had fifteen dozen good-sized fish for one day's catch, and the sport throughout had been excellent. Should any amateur hooker wish to try his luck at the same spot he will find an abundance of boats, bait, and men at Ramsgate and Broadstairs, and an hour's sail on the sea will bring him to very good fishing ground.

Had I racked my brains to find out a hooking spot quite different from the North Foreland, I could not have hit upon a better station than off the Black Rock. There the scenery, the sea even, and the fish, above all, were quite of new kinds. The great cliffs towered majestically over pretty deep water; the bottom was quite rough and rocky, the sea very turbulent, and the fish, which, by-the-way, abounded at every one of our moorings, were all rock fishes. Not a single dab did I see, but congers, pouting, brills, and gurnards were evidently holding a public meeting there.

I am always very partial to rocky bottoms, because, provided one can stand the sea, which at such places has always a pretty heavy ground swell, one is tolerably certain of having good sport. Each recurring tide must displace some of the lighter rocks or stones; and the larger ones (probably cracked in their fall from the heights) eventually must be split quite asunder by the repeated assaults of the heavy waves. Each of these operations brings to the fish a new field of action. Worms are brought to light. Caverns for the smaller species of fish are suddenly uncovered, and their inhabitants, hitherto secure enough, are ready to fall a prey to bigger ones.

In this wise I found my way to the Black Rock. I was going to Brighton, simply for Brighton itself. I intended seeing first the lions, *i.e.* the fishes and the guillemots at the Aquarium; but when I reached the promenade by the sea, and saw a few boats out with pleasure parties, I could not resist the temptation. I walked down to the shingle, and in five minutes I too was out on the brine. It was a cold but fine day, and the sea a little rippled, just as it should be. The Black Rock stands about a mile and a half from the East Pier. It is the home of many sea-birds, and many rooks seem to affect also its "suburbs."

We were about half an hour under weigh, and dropped our stone just opposite the very highest part of the rock at the beginning of the Chain. My men had, of course, the usual coarse tackle. The lines were simply made of stout string, I believe, and the usual wire chopsticks stuck out on each side of the heavy conical leads. The hooks, however, were fair, and picking out amongst the lot the line I fancied best, I baited it and dropped it overboard, becoming aware during the performance of this operation that some half-a-dozen knots or so were gracefully disposed on the handiest part of the line, so that when it was once wet it behoves the holder to be careful in not letting it run freely between his fingers, unless he wished to send bits of his skin as well to the bottom of the sea. My lead had reached bottom I thought, and I was feeling it steadily, when it suddenly ran down again. Evidently it had alighted on the top of a rock, and a wave had washed it off. Presently there came such a bashful bite that I made sure it was a crab, so shook the line merely; but as the something had got on and would not let go, I hauled up and found a little whiting pouting, about four inches long. All the colours of the rainbow were on his coat as he came out of his element, and when the sun shone on him he looked like a piece of silver dotted with precious stones. I turned him loose, of course. My next catch was a gurnard, also a small one.

Presently, as I was lighting a cigar, a violent tug came

on my left hand, round which I had twisted the line. "You have got a good one this time, sir," said the man, and I hastened to look him up—a fine brill, with much perverseness of temper. Instead of coming over the gun'ale decently, it gave a slanting dash, when just about a yard from my hand, and dived actually like a slate on the run, under our keel. Fortunately the tackle was sufficiently strong, and master brill, looking thoroughly disgusted, found himself next moment on the flooring of our boat. Meanwhile, the youngest of my men was hauling up, too, forward, and his catch proved to be a good gurnard and a crab. He was going to crush the latter under the heel of his boot, when I remonstrated with him on the wastefulness of the proceeding. "Don't kill it," I said, "perhaps it is in spawn." "Perhaps it is, sir," said the young fellow. "You are quite right. I never thought of that. But the fact is, if we return them to the sea they come again to one's baits and worry one so." "Well, don't return him until we give up fishing," I suggested. "Here, turn him adrift under the flooring, and if more are caught we will turn them all adrift again at the finish." All sea fishermen ought to act as we did. We were not much annoyed by crabs, however, on our sittings before the Black Rock, as we had but seven or eight to hunt after when we had done. We had very good sport, and were favoured with most lovely weather throughout.

My trip to the North Foreland and that to the Black Rock were the two extremes in the same kind of sport. In one I had rain almost from beginning to end, and warm weather withal. At the other the weather was cold, bracy, and dry. At the first sand-fish were caught. At the other rock-fish. The one had not a single seaweed, the other abounded with it. The Foreland fish were so "good," and the ground so open that not a hook was lost, but at the Black Rock disaster followed upon disaster, and that so fast that soon we were at a standstill for want of hooks. Thus, perforce, was my trip to Black Rock brought to an untimely end. Three dozen good fish, however, was not a bad creel for three hours' fishing, and the next time I chance to be in that neighbourhood I will sit down for a good hooking treat, with sufficient hooks and tackle to stand a very strong run.

OFF THE SOUND.

I MENTIONED in my last chapter the catch of three garfish off the North Foreland. Since then I have met and conversed with an enthusiastic amateur, who does most of his sea-fishing between the North and South Forelands, making Deal and Ramsgate alternately his headquarters. He told me that this year has been quite exceptional as regards garfish. They are rarely caught higher than the English Channel, at least in any quantities, but this season he has seen more than he had ever noticed before, and, strange to say, from all quarters I hear the news. In fact, the mackerel netters and hookers catch more garfish than mackerel just now.

These fish, which are rather despised on this side of the Channel, find a very ready and profitable sale on the other. The French are fond of extraordinary edibles, and I am told that the decidedly obnoxious smell and taste of "long-noses" have found immense favour with them.

A friend who is now in Paris writes me that the *restaurateurs* in fashionable parts of the town cut off the long-noses' bills, and serve them up as lampreys! charging enormous prices for the luxury. We know that "the sauce makes the fish," but surely the villanous natural smell and taste of gar-fish would need a considerable deal of condiment to render it as palatable as the flesh of lampreys.

My Deal friend told me that a shoal of mackerel and gar-fish had paid a visit to the Foreland and two boats which chanced to be out then did very well. He caught only a dozen, and would not catch any more. The boat, he declared, had retained their "perfume" ever since. And a very disagreeable "perfume" it is, as I can personally testify, for, hearing that extraordinary catches were being secured on the coast of Devon, a friend of mine wished to go there, and induced me to go with him, and we spent two days sailing off Plymouth Sound, when we found that the shoals were simply teeming.

We arrived at about five A.M. at Plymouth, and as we had slept well in the train, we simply went to secure a good breakfast, and then at once made tracks for the harbour. We had decided to go so suddenly that I had not been able to send word to the men I know at Plymouth, and we found that they were out to sea. We therefore engaged two other men. They were just going to sea on their "own hook," so that every requisite was ready. As soon as we were fairly under weigh we prepared ourselves for a spin. For sailing I invariably use Hearder's sensitive sinker (as it is called), than which no better can be devised, and I have often wondered how it was that people did not invent it the moment they began sailing. Formerly, it will be remembered that the lead for a railing line was simply an elongated cylinder, tapering at both ends, and ending there by two eyes. To the top eye the line proper was fastened, and to the bottom one the snood was secured.

To avoid the lines kinking, it was usual to rig either on the line or on the snood, and often on both, small brass swivels, which counteracted the spinning motion which the travelling of the boat was sure to communicate to the lead. Certainly the lines thus rigged worked pretty well, and when the boat did not sail too fast, and the fisherman was delicate in his handling of the line, he could almost always tell when he had a bite, but generally he had a good many "false starts." Thus, when the yacht, dipping into the trough of two large waves, rises over the last one, she generally remains almost stationary for a short time, until her sails catch again the full strength of the breeze, and getting over the top of the wave, its resistance to the progress of the hull is lessened, and she may again forge ahead.

During this temporary stoppage any one accustomed to sailing will bear in mind that the lead, no longer pulling against the impetus of the vessel, drops to the bottom, if the stoppage is long enough, or drops towards the bottom, at any rate. Then, when the yacht gathers way again, the lead is sheared upwards once more to its proper height. Whilst doing so the lead, according to the new impetus of the yacht, always jumps more or less, and with the old system of lines it jumped so very neatly that the inexperienced sea-fisherman was almost sure to call out that he had a fish, haul up his line hopefully, and find that he was mistaken. With Hearder's improved arrangement no such mistakes can very well arise if everything is properly adjusted. Of course the lead will jump just the same, but the jumping is rendered quite distinct from the bite of a fish. This end is arrived at by having the elongated lead made hollow throughout its length. Through the hole is thrust a brass pin, about half an inch, or even a quarter of an inch only, longer than the lead. Then both ends of the pin are turned over to form two eyes, and two swivels are fixed to these eyes. The line is then secured to one of them, and the snood to the other. In work then, it will be found that any jumping of the lead will be readily detected, and any bite will be felt quite distinctly even if the fish should bite just when the boat starts forward. Thus during our trip in and off the Sound I frequently told my companion that I had a fish or two, and once I had three, and said so before hauling the line, simply because I could feel when the bites were taking place. The brass pin makes the communication between the hooks and the hand of the hooker direct and complete; in short, it is just as if one had only a plain line in hand. The moment a fish makes a rush he pulls on a hook, and the brass pin being jerked through the lead offers no impediment to the information being communicated to the fisherman, whereas with the old system there was often ground for doubting whether the fish was on or whether it was only a false alarm.

The only thing I find yet troublesome about the sinkers is this, and I commend it to the attention of the makers. It frequently happens that a man has a favourite flight of flies and spinner with which he thinks he can kill better than with any other. When such is the case—supposing the lead chances to be too light or too heavy, according to the rate at which the yacht or boat is sailing—it is very awkward to change the said lead. A deal of precious time is wasted, and, to say the least, it is not entertaining.

True, one might take a fresh line, with a heavier or lighter lead, according as the state of affairs may require; but then, as I observed before, when one likes a particular line one likes to stick to it, and besides, there may not be any other line handy.

Would it not be well, therefore, to make the eyes of the brass pins rather larger than they are, so as to be able to rig the said pins on the lines and on the snoods by means of small spring hooks? If this were done, see how handy it would be when one might wish to alter the lead. In half a moment a fresh one could be substituted. Should any maker work out the alteration, he will confer a boon on sea-fishermen. I would not confine that system to railing lines only, but I would have it extended to all lines with which leads are employed.

When at anchor, for instance, a deep-sea line is rendered frequently quite useless when a strong tide sets in and disturbs the bottom of the sea, unless the lead be very heavy. Heavy leads are only to be employed when they are absolutely necessary. The lighter leads are, the better; therefore it is rather a nuisance, when one is peacefully hooking with a light lead, to find that, owing to a stream of tide setting strong, he will have to haul up his line and take another one with a heavier lead, or else alter the lead of his original line.

In the latter case the knife has to be used, and time and care are wanted to make the alteration. Should, however, the end of the line be garnished with a swivel spring-hook and the top of the lead with an eye, in an instant one could work the alteration with comfort, speed, and certainty.

To return, however, to my trip. By-the-way, we were told by our boatman that many bass were about, and I remember well catching a few myself there some time back; but on the trip I am now narrating we only caught one, and that reminded me of " Pelagius's " grievance about bass catching, as once narrated in *Bell*.

Bass are extraordinary fish, certainly, and I verily believe that if you make up your mind to go bass-fishing, you will catch anything else but bass. At least that is my experience. In fact, there are so many atmospheric and other circumstances to be depended upon, that it is much safer not to think too much of the bass, but fish on for anything, and thank your stars when bass condescend to notice your bait.

I may, however, here state that bass will take more especially sand eels or an artificial spinner rigged out for pollock, when the fit comes into their heads. The lonely one we caught took the spinner like a crocodile, shaking it well, though it was not a big fish. We caught it on our return journey, at dusk.

The first fish we caught was a gurnard, also on the spinner. He was not a large one, but his mouth was (like the mouth of a sack) as broad as his middle, and as he stood gaping at us, we could not help criticising his build. This fish had not made a rush at the spinner. He had, I believe, taken advantage of a momentary lull in our progress, in order to try to swallow it, taking it, we doubt not, for a nice bit of mackerel or other " bright " fish.

At first I did not know what to make of it, as he allowed himself to be hauled along through the water, without offering any resistance.

"I believe I have got hold of some seaweeds," I said ; but when I pulled up the line astern the fish jumped up, and we saw him. But gurnards frequently take the bait even when in rapid motion.

Whilst I was clearing my line, my companion said :

"Look at that ripple on the sea ahead of us! We shall have a breeze presently."

We turned round to look, and our man instantly eased his boat.

"It is a shoal of mackerel, mister," said he; "you will have bites in a moment."

The words were hardly out of his mouth, when my friend had a tug, jerked his line, and the fish went with lightning-like motions. In the midst of his evolutions another fish hooked himself, so that he had two for his first haul—both splendid fish.

Mackerel are simply superb when just taken out of the sea, and I wonder none of our clever fish artists try to depict them in all their pristine beauties. I made all speed to emulate my friend's deeds, and by a judicious slight pull induced a couple to gobble up and be hooked. They were so close to us (I had the short line with the lightest lead, so as not to entangle our lines) that we could see the whole affair. The sea was clear, and at first we could see nothing therein. Suddenly there appeared three or four very dark greenbacks, darting like arrows towards the silver spinner, and lo! two of the greenbacks showed their silver bellies, and made frantic efforts to be off, but it was "no go."

My next catch numbered three, and had I not been in a hurry to get them in, I believe I should have hooked one more, for he passed quite close to the last fish when I was hauling up, and evidently was intent on feeding.

We were then at the mouth of the Sound, and the weather being quite calm, we ventured out, and went in for a regular hook-and-line sail for gar-fish. My friend had never had any gar-fish on his line, and was anxious to know what they were like.

"You will soon see," quoth I, "as the men are taking us to the shoals."

For some time we did not catch one. For about an hour that we kept on tacking and railing, we only caught mackerel, and not many either, but when we got about five miles from the Lighthouse the fun began. I had had a strong wrench and was pulling in, when up went a gar-fish in the air, about a yard above the sea.

"Saw him?" I inquired of my companion.

"Yes," he said, "an eel, is it not?"

"A queer sort of eel, mister," said our helmsman; "that was a long-nose. Them fish always jump in that style."

At last, then, here was the chance for him to see a gar-fish, but fate was against us, for just when I was getting it well over, the fish opened his beak and—was gone. Almost immediately after my friend got one. He handled it very gingerly, and positively declined to touch it when he got it on board. Discretion is certainly the better part of valour. Our second man then came forward, looking unspeakably contemptuous. He flopped the two-foot long sole of his sea-boat over the head of the long-nose, dexterously opened its jaws, unhooked the spinner, and pitched the fish in a tub. My friend left his line to go and examine the long-nose. He soon had to hold his handkerchief to his own nose.

"What a villanous smell!" said he; "how can anyone eat such a beast! And look here, he goes on wriggling all over the tub, and has painted it green with his scales."

The gar-fish bit well throughout the day. After luncheon we got nearly three dozen long-noses, besides about as many mackerel. I need not remark that we kept them apart.

In the evening, on our return journey, we caught another dozen fish or so, including the solitary bass, and that concluded the day's sport.

We had a good dinner at an hotel to make up for previous deficiencies in our victualling department, and intended taking a stroll through the town, but the heat of the dining-room overpowered us, and we nearly went off to sleep over our cigars.

Next morning we were disinclined to stir very early, but at ten o'clock we turned up for our breakfasts. The waiter told us that there was excellent mullet-fishing to be had near the docks, several residents having made extraordinary creels of them, but I knew that every good point of vantage would be taken by the natives. A lot of boats had turned in harbour early, we were further informed, and some of them had made some grand catches with the drift-nets for mackerel.

We went to look for our men, and when we reached the harbour found the boat at her moorings, and no one attending her. We took another boat, whose skipper charged us about double the usual, and already pretty liberal, fee. We took the can of bait we had purchased, but not used, the day before, and away we went, whiffing all the way, with pretty fair results, until we were a couple of miles out at sea, when we came to an anchor to try bottom-fishing. The scene was very pretty. There was the lighthouse on our starboard, behind us stretched the shore, and in the offing were the fishing-smacks hard at work, some with their nets shot, others taking them up, and a few crowding, with all sail set, into the Sound, to take their catches to market. The sea was not so smooth as on the previous day, a strong ground swell having set in which made my companion feel rather squeamish. Still, he held out bravely.

It was nearly three P.M. when we had reached our fishing-ground; we had, therefore, little more than three or four hours' daylight left us, and as we had plenty of bait I did not spare it. The result was that I got together about the best and most varied catch of fish I had had for some time. Congers were beginning to show up well, and I had three of very respectable size, besides others of only two or three pounds. I got several splendid gurnards, two large brill, three small ones, several very fine pouting, two skates, and an enormous quantity of crabs, &c.

The sea then began to get rougher; the wind rose; my companion turned yellow, blue, and green, and looked dying. I thought it best to get under shelter, and our men picked up our moorings, and sailed us back to the Sound, where we found the sea much smoother. The mackerel and gar-fish were still on the feed. The latter especially meant business, and they flew at the bright baits like arrows. This augured rough weather in store, argued our men; and sure enough, just when it got dark, it began to blow and rain in squalls, when, as if by magic, all the sails we had seen out began to appear, one behind the other, making for harbour. The sport throughout our trip was excellent.

IN THE DOWNS AND OFF THE SOUTH FORELAND.

IN accordance with the programme we had set forth, we laid in provisions and set sail from Gravesend for a trip to the Needles. But the north-west wind, which sent the yacht spinning along down old Father Thames, and would have answered tolerably, at any rate, in the Channel, veered downright west before we had been four hours under sail, and it remained so steady in that quarter that nothing remained but to put off our original trip, choose some suitable spot, and see what was to be done there. We had started at four P.M., and kept under sail all night. I took my share of the work until midnight, when I went below, and when I turned up the next morning at seven o'clock we were passing Ramsgate, and the Gull light-vessel was on our bows.

The morning looked squally and rainy, and the day proved a mixture, for we had alternately a shower, sunshine, a blow, a lull, another shower, another peep of the sun for half an hour at a stretch, and so on. My new companion (a reader of *Bell*, who had wished to join me) was at first rather disgusted with that state of things, but the next day made amends. Now when the season for coarse fish is over, I would recommend anglers, by way of change, to see what consolation the sport of sea-fishing might have in store for them. I do not remember a better year for sea-fishing than this one proved to be.

The weather throughout the winter had been so mild that the breeding had not been interfered with, and that is a very great consideration. Every sea-coast resident knows that in hard winters tons upon tons of fish are killed by the frost and thrown ashore. This being so, most of the fry must suffer in the same manner; but the fry being small, the loss is not so readily perceptible. It is, however, none the less severely felt when the fishing season begins.

To give an instance to the point. In the winter of 1870–1871, I remember seeing on the sands hundreds of large fish of sundry species quite dead, frozen to death, in fact and of course many smaller fish or fry escaped detection. A broad statement of the variety we caught in the Downs and off the South Foreland may tempt some holiday-makers to try the spots. Well, then, we had loads of fish, comprising plaice, dabs, mackerel, soles, turbot, whiting, gurnards, skate, and small cod.

In honour of our new companion we had brought long lines, on the principle that, being a new hand, he would probably delight in seeing many fish caught. We had not a parcel of bait, and thought at first of running into Ramsgate to secure some; but, spying some fishermen about, we sailed to them, and asked them to spare us some bait.

At first the man at the helm shook his head very doubtfully. "Got none to spare," said he gruffly.

"What is the row?" asked another voice, in an

authoritative manner, from the smack's smoky cabin, and two more hands turned up.

"Genelmen as wants bait," explained the first speaker.

"Well, it all depends what they will give for it," rejoined the skipper; and, turning to us, "We have got mussel and crabs and a few lugs. Can spare you this 'ere large tin full for a crown. Will that do?"

Well, of course it was, to some extent, Hobson's choice. True, we might have run into harbour, but searching for bait is like the proverbial wild-goose chase.

We did not hesitate a moment, and were very glad to clinch the bargain. So our Scotchman, with the crown, went into the dinghy and rowed to the smack, where he got the tin fairly crammed for the money.

We were now provided with all we wanted, and with light hearts we set about preparing the long lines. We had three, each with a hundred hooks on, and each of us—the owner, our new friend, and I—took one in hand.

In the midst of our preparation, our friend said, pointing over our starboard: "What is that sort of fort yonder?"

"Sandwich Battery," I replied, "and, by-the-way, some one told me that bass are to be had in Pegwell Bay. Shall we stop and go back to it now, or first set our long lines, and then see about the bass?"

It was agreed that, since we had begun baiting, we might as well finish it, and then come back again. Wherever bass are announced, sea-fishermen, as a rule, will try their luck there, on the principle, I believe, that what is hard to get is worth trying for.

We came to an anchor a little below the Gull light-vessel, and forthwith the dinghy was in great requisition. We placed our lines carefully at the bottom of the little craft, and in the midst of a regular Scotch mist rowed away towards Trinity Bay, where our hand declared that he knew a first-rate spot. When we arrived at the right place I volunteered to take the oars and do the rowing, provided he undertook to pay out the lines. We then rowed to the yacht, set sail back, had luncheon meanwhile, and then set out in the dinghy to try for bass.

This time the hand remained on board, the three of us going by ourselves. Our friend took a scull, I took the other, and the owner standing astern with his back to us, began his railing. He tried a spoon, a moderate-sized one, not over bright, and did not get a single bite.

"Perhaps sailing would answer better," quoth he; "I believe the splashing of the oars frightens away the fish."

"Let us row up towards land," I replied, "and then set up the mast and sail, and we will sail back quietly." No sooner said than done.

Meanwhile I advised him to change the spoon, as the plating was quite gone in some places. He rigged on a brand-new one, we rowed up, and sailed back, and we all tried our hands with spoon and with minnow without effect.

At last we gave it up, and went back, the "hand" grinning under his sou'-wester when he saw no fish. "Ah," he said, "there is nothing in this 'ere world like a long line in *my* estimation. You baits the hooks, you pays out the lines, you comes aboard to get your dinner, you smokes a pipe arterwards, and drinks a glass or two, comfortable like, or goes to sleep; and then you goes to your lines, picks 'em up, and there you are."

We had been a couple of hours on our bass-catching (?) trip, and as the long lines had been altogether about four hours set, we made up our minds to take them up. Speculation ran brisk the moment we began to consider how many fish we should have.

"If we have one fish for every ten hooks," I explained to our companion, "we ought to feel satisfied."

"Ay, ay, sir," said the yacht sailor; "it will be a very fair catch if we have that much."

I had to explain to our friend that the lines being left alone such a long time, no doubt many fish which have hooked themselves slightly, get off. I assured him that if we had ten fair fish on each line it would be satisfactory.

He persisted that there would be more, and "I will bet you a dinner at an hotel at Deal," said he, "that we get at least sixty good fish."

"Done!" I answered; and we went to get the lines up.

"I feel one—a good one," said our man when he began, and with the second hook came a large dab.

"One!" he called out.

Next came a gurnard, "two!" then a pouting, "three!" then another dab, then a codling, then a plaice, then a whiting, then nothing for a long interval of at least thirty hooks; then a large cod, and next to him a monstrous gray gurnard. The rest was made up of rubbish, crabs, &c.—total, nine fish for the first line.

I made sure of success, and we went to the first buoy of the second line.

"The line is heavy," said Tom, the moment he got the little anchor up· "there's a good haul on this one, sir."

At that piece of news my companion began rubbing his hands, and telling me what dishes he would have me to stand, in the treat in store for him. To make matters short, I won the bet, but with about ten fish only.

By the time the whole lot were aboard it was getting quite dark. The ships in the Downs were lighting up their riding-lights for the night, and as we intended going to Deal, we had to get our own lights up. We were about an hour under sail ere we got fairly abreast of the pier, and before the sails were taken in and everything made taut and snug for the night, it was nearly eight o'clock, and I need not add that three more hungry souls seldom trod the deck of a ten-tonner before.

We rowed ashore to the pier, and there confided the dinghy to an old salt who was waiting for a job of some sort, and then wended our way towards an hotel. The wind, meanwhile, moderated considerably, the clouds went their way, the moon rose, and when we came out after dinner, the night was as peaceful and as lovely as anyone could wish.

Our friend thereupon, who had intended sleeping ashore and joining us in the morning, made up his mind to come back with us; so when we arrived at the yacht we had to extemporise a shake-down for him on the middle of the cabin floor.

By a very welcome contrast our second day was the very opposite of the preceding one. We did not get a drop of rain, and the sun shone over the sea for considerably the best part of the day. We set sail at dawn of day, and the novelty of the thing seemed to impress our friend very much. We were bound this time to the South Sand Head, and passed Walmer Castle at about seven, Kingsdown at half-past, and with the South Calliper well on our port side, we headed for the light-ship, and came to an anchor about half a mile lower.

We had at Deal secured a pailful of lugs, and meant having our money's worth out of them; so we rigged out the long lines once more, and forthwith went to lay them. This done, we set sail, and went railing towards St. Margaret, and as far as the South Foreland lighthouses, meeting with very good sport at mackerel and gar-fish. After a couple of hours of this we went back to lift the lines, as we meant laying them again in another spot. We had a moderately fair catch on the first, a worse one on the second; but the last one had about thirty fish.

This was satisfactory; but I knew the neighbourhood of the Beacon, about six or seven miles higher, in a north-easterly direction, would be still better. So we sought out a chart, and our owner set sail to make it out. This Beacon, called Trinity Beacon on the charts, stands about three miles across the Goodwin Sands, and just opposite Trinity Bay.

The man being busy cooking dinner, we thought it would be wrong to disturb him, so we went by ourselves, and I am not likely to forget that little expedition. Just as we were starting my friend said he would row, as he was cold. Accordingly, I sat astern in the dinghy, whilst he stepped forward and took his seat. Now, the flat lids on which the long lines were coiled, ready to be shipped and rigged with anchors and bladders, were dispersed a little everywhere (those lines take a deal of room), and what should my worthy companion do but upset one of the lids, thereby entangling the line thereon coiled to an unlimited extent, and when trying to save its fall, he sat on one of

In the Downs and off the South Foreland. 225

the oars, which, chancing to be underneath the next lid on the stern seat, tilted it bodily over the gun'ale, and it was gone—anchors, bladders, and line—in irretrievable confusion! We looked at each other with dismay.

"Let us drag for it," I suggested, "with one of the other sinkers; but first let us see if the bladders won't rise to the surface."

We all looked and looked, until at last I saw, about a fathom from the surface, one of the bladders. Evidently it was getting clear of the wreck, and, by gently helping it with one of the oars, we eventually got it up, and I seized it.

"Now, gently does it, sir," quoth the yacht sailor, standing astern on the yacht; "for please bear in mind that both sinkers are probably weighing on the bladder line, and if that line should break, we should never see the rest of the concern."

At my request he joined us, and I relinquished the line to him, and right well did he rescue it.

"The two anchors," said he, as he was hauling up hand over hand, "is a comin' together. Will you take hold on it. If we can get hold of one of 'em we are safe."

Well, I looked over the gun'ale, and seizing the first sinker, I found that the second was close to it, held by one of its flukes in a loop, and of course we got the line and all, but what a mess it was in! We left the wrecked line on board the yacht, and without further mishap, went to drop the two others.

We then went hand-line fishing. I remained in the dinghy, finding it more comfortable to fish from there, and we all got on very well until the tide came up with such violence that the dinghy sheared from port to starboard, and *vice versa*, with such pulls that I really thought the painter would give way. There was no hooking possible then, as, no matter how heavy our leads were, the lines would go yards away from us before reaching bottom. Moreover, when such a stream sets on, the fish are scared, and the sport began to get very slack. We therefore thought we had better drop it, and go to ascertain how the two other lines were getting on. We found about two score of fish caught, all the hooks bare, two were broken clean off, and one snood gone *in toto*. Dog-fish had done the damage evidently. One of them was caught, but he was too small to have so broken our tackle.

This brought an end to our fishing. It was getting dark, we had had our fill of railing and of hooking, and we rather longed to be ashore again after our sea-trip. It was arranged that the Needles trip should be carried out the following week, and the yacht would be sailed either to Ramsgate or to Dover, or even lower on the south coast if possible, I to join her by rail, and then we would sail for the Isle of Wight. Of course this would all depend on the weather.

FROM PORTSMOUTH TO THE NEEDLES.

A MAN must be very hard to please who cannot find enjoyment in sea-fishing, especially if he is, when engaged in that pursuit, on board a sailing boat. Besides the pleasure of hooking, an ever-changing panorama is before his eyes, particularly should he chance to be cruising about the Isle of Wight. There are so many different points of view to be admired, and the landscape is now and then so fascinating that one's mind gets wholly absorbed in its contemplation. Such were my thoughts the other day during our trip to the Needles.

We started early from Portsmouth, where I had come by rail to join the yacht, and a more pleasant trip it has rarely been my lot to enjoy. Early as the hour was, some enthusiastic amateur sea-fishermen were already at work on the pier. Sitting on the stairs, lines in hand, creels by their side, and bait-can within reach, was a family of hookers—father and three sons—hard at it, and laughing and enjoying the breeze and the sunshine and the sport. The youngsters were having a fine time of it, the fish biting well and bringing them no end of pleasure.

Some boys, by-the-way, are extremely clever at hooking,

and one of those I am speaking of, whom I had the pleasure of watching for five minutes, was as expert in the art as anyone I have yet seen. He hooked every time, and never gave a false start, but one could see that his whole soul was in it. They were all using ordinary lines, as far as the sinker and line were concerned, but the usual wire chopsticks had been sensibly dispensed with, and the snoods, three in number, were fixed, at intervals of a foot or so from the lead, to short whalebone or wooden sticks, kept at right angles with the line by bits of string. Their hooks were rather small and baited with mussel, and the pouting seemed to appreciate the luxury very heartily, for the little fellows were hauling them up as fast as could be.

The breeze was favourable for our expedition, and the moment I got on board away flew the yacht, getting her cabin combings almost under. We were going too fast for railing, so I quietly enjoyed the journey. As we wanted to make as short a passage as possible, our helmsman got orders to shave Gilliker Point, and then to hold a straight course for Cowes. Within half an hour we passed the Point, and finding ahead of us another yacht, also in cruising trim, we clapped on all sail in chase, but she held her own, and finally she got into Cowes Harbour, her evident destination. The wooded slopes of the coast, illumined by the bright sun, were inexpressibly charming, and the old town of Cowes seemed as busy as usual.

We had been three hours only coming across, and as we turned into the Solent the wind was right astern then, and the way the yacht "hummed" told tales.

At noon we passed Newtown Bay, at half-past one Yarmouth, and with the Hurst Castle on our starboard we rounded into Colwell Bay, where we had to change our tack, as we wanted then to hug the shore pretty close. When we reached Heatherwood Point, we began to slacken the main-sheet, and holding up fairly for the Needles, we commenced railing for mackerel. Several trawlers and hookers were in Christchurch Bay at work, some four or five miles from us, and a good many vessels taking advantage of the opening of the weather and fair wind, were scudding along under full sail in the Channel. These, and a few bright-coloured steamers, made the scene look quite lively.

For my railing I used a spinner and a flight of flies, supplemented by a piece of mackerel skin, and having rigged my spinning apparatus according to the hints I gave in one of my preceding chapters, I found that I could at will alter either the sinker or the spinner without losing a minute.

On the other hand, I found that the spring hooks, although when the line is fairly extended they answer admirably, will not do if the lead rests at all, as the swivels then are apt to go upwards into the spring-hooks, and clog their springs. It is, however, but a minor defect, albeit it does not look well, though I daresay it could easily be remedied. A little half-ring, to be inserted at the opening of the spring-hook, would doubtless hold the swivel in its place, and prevent it getting into the spring.

Strange to say, to begin with, five times running I caught mackerel on the mackerel skin, the flies being untouched, though after awhile they came at us fast and furiously, and I hooked as quickly as I could wish for about half an hour. Getting opposite the Needles, and setting full sail for the cliffs, we came to an anchor for a little ground-fishing. Here, again, the bottom lines showed the desirability of some arrangement being devised to keep spring-hooks and swivels in order, though on the whole we progressed remarkably well, and it did not materially interfere with sport.

The place we chose to anchor in was between the Old Pepper Rock and the Sun Point, about one mile from the shore. We had a rare lot of fresh bait, and having placed our tubs handy for the reception of fish we began, my two friends and I, whilst the sailor went below to prepare our dinner. I thought I would set a drift line, on the off chance of hooking a good fish, whilst hand-line hooking, after the manner of many sea fishermen who use drift-lines, on account of their being so very handy that they positively require little or no attendance. These lines consist simply of forty fathoms of hair-line, at the end of which are rigged a strong snood and two yards of good gut, for the hook and bait. To sink this line a lot of pipe leads are ready threaded on the hair line, and each lead is provided with a little wooden peg, cut at one end whistle-fashion, which being inserted at either end of the pipe leads, and thrust into it, presses against the line, and thus keeps the lead stationary wherever set. In this fashion one may slip down to the snood as many leads as may be required according to the speed the stream of the tide is running. Some men distance these pipe leads, having sometimes an interval of a yard or more between them; but it will be found that when that arrangement is adopted a great deal of bother is experienced by the fisherman when he hauls up his line, as he is apt then to knock off the pegs and lose them, or else they catch on the gun'ale when being brought up. I therefore adopt the far more simple plan of just slipping down in a lump two, three, four, or more leads, and securing the top and bottom ones fixes the lot all in one place, rendering the taking up of the line as easy as that of any other line, and I experience no difficulty in the way the line "sets" in the sea. The main point is to calculate to a nicety how many "shots" one will require; that is all the secret.

In the position we had taken up there was but little stream at the time, and calculating that, the tide being slack, there would not be required a great deal of weight to sink it, I slipped down three of the pipe leads, secured them by their pegs, baited the hook with a good-sized lugworm, and I cast it adrift, paying it out as it went, until the whole line was stretched. This done, I secured it, and then attended to my hand-hooking.

My companions were having but moderate sport, as the fish caught were mostly small, as the larger ones evidently were waiting for an appetite, and it at last came, for we had afterwards an excellent run. I had a large brill on, and lost it, the snood breaking just when the handsome fish was getting out of the sea. A moment afterwards the owner exclaimed that he had caught it, and proceeding cautiously, taught by my lesson I suppose, he landed his fish, but it was not the one I had previously hooked. Our friend then caught a conger, I hooked a pouting, then he had a brill, and I had again a pouting. In short, poutings seemed to have a partiality for my lines, for I caught no less than a score before darkness set in.

Congers began to show up well, a few being, moreover, of very decent size, but they are a terrible nuisance when caught, and it is no joke having to deal with two or three at the same time in a narrow cockpit. We were that way occupied when the man, coming up on deck, called out that a fish was on the drift line. We turned round, and I seized the line, but no sooner had I begun pulling than a small diver came up, energetically fluttering, on the surface of the sea. It was he who was hooked, and the man had seen him when he was just diving.

"Try to catch him," said my friends, and I tried my best; but the bird was wide-awake, and as soon as he felt the tug he resisted to the utmost, and finally got clear off. I suppose that whilst we were all stooping over our congers in the cockpit the bird had come near the boat, thinking nobody was about, and having in his diving seen the bait, had gone down after it and gobbled it up. I have hooked several divers when out sea-fishing, but these incidents have always happened in very severe weather. Thus, once in Kingston Harbour I hooked a grebe twice in succession, and at the second attempt I got it in my boat, but it disgorged the bait, and scrambled over the gun'ale before I could seize it. On the Continent, however, there are many coastmen who regularly set baited hooks for them at sea, and not unfrequently they catch half-a-dozen or even more at one tide.

As soon as the drift-line was again let out we resumed our bottom-fishing, and scarcely had the tide carried the bait a good distance out than a fish jumped up, about a foot over the waves, in the direction it had taken, and I opined that fish (whatever it was) had swallowed the bait, and as a matter of course found the hook, and in desperation begun an acrobatic performance. This guess was an excellent "shot" at the truth, and on pulling the line the fish, four or five times in succession, repeated his performances, and then we found it was a garfish—our first of the day.

This strong-smelling gentleman being bagged, adrift again went the line, baited this time with a piece of mackerel. Hardly is it paid out when another tug comes to it. I seize the line as it rests on the gun'ale, feel it, and the welcome tug, tug, tug, proclaims another catch.

"The drift-line has all the luck," quoth one of my companions, and when I declare the newcomer to be a mackerel, the railing lines are at once in great demand, and our man is called upon to set sail. I hastily rig out a short rod whilst he is preparing to slacken the sheets. I fix a spinner and five or six flies as quickly as possible, and then make a throw in the direction where we had caught with the drift-line; but there I am nonplussed, for the wind is dead against that performance, and, in fact, it blows the silver spinner and the flies all over the yacht, and the hooks get in a mess with the rigging.

Evidently the line wants doctoring. I have in my tackle box some bullet-sinkers, with holes pierced through them. I pick out one of these, which weighs about half an ounce, and unrigging the flight of flies, I just slip the line through the hole in the bullet, then I refasten the flight, and I am quite ready. The moment I take up the rod and give the preliminary swing for a cast, I find the spinner and the rest perfectly under control, and the weight of the bullet, augmented by the impulsion, fairly counteracts the tendency of the wind to throw the line back in my teeth.

I made a good throw, some thirty yards or so, and instantly began working the flies against the ripple. Tug. "That is one!" called I, in great glee.

"What! one already?" ask my companions in a breath.

"Yes," I reply.

Another tug. "Here is another."

And, as I haul up, tug again.

"Well, I have got three now, or I am much mistaken."

And sure enough, three lovely mackerel make their appearance. It was getting dusk, and the shoals were positively teeming and ravenous. And what fun it was! My rod was describing all sorts of figures under their pressure, and it was rather a treat to have a bite every time a throw was made almost. Garfish and mackerel, mackerel and garfish, on they came, until the cockpit, the buckets, and the deck were alive and slimy with the lot.

The mackerel die as soon as caught, but the garfish are not so tender, and the way they crawled here, there, and everywhere, was a nuisance.

By-and-by, in the midst of the fun, and to our great astonishment, the man came up with the riding-lamp, and we looked up surprised, and found that darkness had invaded the sky and blackened the sea. We had been so intent on our rod-and-line sport that night actually had taken us all by surprise. The cabin-lamp had been lighted, the cloth was laid, and Tom announced officially: "Denner be ready, gentlemen."

There was no going against that. The cold night air had somewhat chilled us, and when the first excitement of the shoals had passed away we began to feel, not only cold, but hungry, and altogether in want of rest. So at the well-timed intimation of the sailor we gladly listened to the "voice of the charmer," and forthwith rod-unjointing became general. Then a grand washing of slimy hands, and we defile through the cockpit into the cabin. There we find the stove roaring itself red-hot; the steaming dishes are handed from forward through the partition, our owner dives his hand into a mysterious locker near the door, and produces therefrom some suspicious-looking bottles of different shapes, and, after a very hearty, and I may say heartfelt, grace before meat, we fell to with a will.

Talk about appetites! The air round the Needles is as sharp as needles, particularly during the evening, and the man who cannot there make a hearty meal must be past all human help.

When dinner drew to an end our next movements were discussed. "If the wind is fair," said our owner, "we can sail to Yarmouth for the night. Cowes is too far, we should be the whole night getting there; and then as soon as we reached the place it would be time to start back.

"But," I said, "do you know Yarmouth at all?"

"No," he replied, "I have never been there."

"Neither have I;" and our friend had not, neither had Tom.

"This being the case, none of us can pilot the boat into the harbour, if there is a harbour, which I doubt," I concluded, "and therefore we might run her ashore, on the shallows, or get into some equally undesirable spot. Now the night is clear; the barometer is 'at fair;' there is no storm likely to overtake us; we are somewhat sheltered here from the wind by the headland; I put it to the vote that we stay here for the night instead of trying to sail to ports totally unknown to us."

"Hear, hear!" said my friends, and Tom at once went on deck to make everything taut.

At six o'clock next morning we were all up on deck with sundry basins, and as soon as our scrubbing was done, and whilst breakfast was being got ready, we dropped three drift-lines overboard, and began overlooking our bait and our fish. Of the latter we picked seven or eight to make part of our breakfast, and our fresh mackerel proved most delicious, probably because we had caught them ourselves.

After breakfast we went under easy sail, running backwards and forwards two or three miles across the Solent, towards Christchurch Bay, and back along the south coast of the Isle of Wight, whiffing all the time until noon. The garfish bit well, and the mackerel, though slack for a time, eventually visited us also very fairly, as we had three dozen before luncheon time. The man, by-the-way, ate *fifteen* (!) for his dinner, in preference to roast beef. After luncheon, to give the man time to clear away and clean things in general, we remained at anchor. We were then in Alum Bay, about half a mile from the Needles, and we caught there a few flat fish, but none very large, so we quietly got up the jib ourselves, and drifted again past the Needles, being anxious to catch something worth our while.

We had two or three pollack near the rocks, with rod, line, and spinner. One of these weighed seven pounds, and judging from the way in which he went towards the bottom when he was hooked I thought he certainly would in some way get clear, either by smashing the gut trace, or the hook, or the line. But a little patient humouring, joined to a very steady hold of the rod, at last mastered the wily fellow, and he was finally gaffed and landed all right. We had several other bites, but they all ended in disaster, the fish being so heavy as to defy our gentle efforts and our fine tackle.

I knew a man who could manage, on single gut, almost any fish; but he was endowed with an amount of patience which has been denied me, and I hold too tight, or cut short the struggle too sharp, ending by losing my fish, and of course it serves me right. But I cannot help it. When anything extra heavy gets on the tackle it is but natural that one should wish to see what it is, especially at sea, where the variety of fish is so great. On a river, for trout or for salmon, one knows what one has on the fly, but at sea it may be a bass, a pollack, or a mackerel, a garfish, a gurnard, a codling, or what not, and when the weight tells of something extraordinary, greediness gets the upper hand over patience and discretion, and the ordinary result is a piece of line left bare and a spinner and flies gone to the bottom of the sea.

We remained fishing (changing our stations every couple of hours) nearly the whole day, and caught a rare lot of fish. At four P.M. we set sail for the return journey. We had a heavy beat to windward to get into the Solent, but having sailed a good four miles into Christchurch Bay, we got there a good reach, and tacking by Hurst Castle, we remained on the starboard tack the whole journey back to Portsmouth, where I landed in the morning to take the train. The second day had not been so fine as the first, but we had had no rain, and this, combined with the beauty of the Isle of Wight coast, rendered our trip to the Needles one thoroughly enjoyable, and I owe many hearty thanks to my genial companions for the treat I enjoyed in their society.

SPITHEAD AND HAYLING ISLAND.

IN this epoch of fast things a man must have some quick and tangible results in everything he undertakes, and sport ranks pre-eminently in that respect. In shooting, large bags are now a necessity; hence battueing, driving, pheasant rearing, and preserving in general, on an extraordinary scale. Nowadays a man does not go rambling over his estate every day throughout the season behind his setters. He breeds, rears, or buys the number of birds he wants, and kills them wholesale.

In angling, something akin to this description of sport will shortly be resorted to, and in a few years we shall hear of streams stocked with trout (and salmon, perhaps) at a few days', or may be hours', notice, whenever the owner or the lessee may wish to invite a few friends for some "flogging" at his water.

But what about sea-fishing? Ay! now *there* is a sport where no man can stock against his coming. He must take his chance against everybody else; and yet, strange to say, he cannot, even if he should try, come home empty-handed. It is almost impossible to have a blank day at sea. Hear that! ye intrepid sportsmen, who go hundreds and thousands of miles for sport, the equal of which you may get at your own doors without even the proverbial "asking." Yes, sirs, whenever you will make up your minds to have a day at sea-fishing I promise you two very important and very satisfactory results—a creel heavily loaded, and a day's enjoyment.

To the salmon and trout angler, clad from head to foot in his waterproof contrivances, and standing any amount of wind, rain, and other unpleasant etceteras—to such an enthusiast I would recommend a trial. Some men, however, who try sea-fishing in a desultory sort of manner meet with little or no success. I have occasionally seen such at work, and the following is the way in which they proceed:

They bait their hooks in such a fashion often that the bait comes off a long time even before the lead reaches the bottom. Then they light their pipes, or read a novel, and look to their lines when they think about it.

Under such circumstances no wonder their catches are small. Then, after spending an hour or two thus employed they come back ashore and say that the fish are not on the feed! Others provide anything for bait, on the principle that, no matter what is on the hook, sea fish are so greedy that they will come to it! Now, this is not the way to do things. See how careful a trout angler is to provide himself with everything he may require; what costly tackle, got up regardless of expense, he uses.

Note, moreover, how enthusiastic he is in his pursuit; he neglects nothing to ensure success, and he meets with success as a matter of course. Now compare with this gallant Knight of the Rod the ordinary manœuvres of a seaside visitor, who for the first time intends doing a little sea-fishing. He will invest altogether the large sum of a shilling in a line and bait, and forthwith goes to the pier-head, catches half-a-dozen fish in half an hour, and if the fish do not bite faster he goes home disgusted. Had he secured proper tackle, and gone into the affair heartily, the probabilities are that he would have enjoyed real fun. But to my tale.

According to our preconcerted arrangements I went down to Portsmouth, where my friends had agreed to remain until my return. I arrived overnight, and in order to be ready for an early start, we all slept aboard. At seven o'clock we were off, passing the pier, and the wind being moderate we took to our whiffing lines at once. We intended sailing across Spithead towards Sea View, in the Isle of Wight, and from thence taking a tack straight for the mouth of Chichester Harbour, where, around Hayling Island, we expected to meet with good sport.

Meanwhile, as very often shoals of mackerel are flying about Spithead, we set three railing lines on "their own hooks," by fixing them to "tell-tales." For the benefit of the beginner, I may as well explain how this is done. To begin with, were the lines to be of the same length, or thereabout, and their leads of the same weight, the lines would not be two minutes in the sea before getting into an almost irretrievable confusion. They would twist around one another, and the hooks, the leads, and lines would defy anything like setting them in proper order under at least a couple of hours of exemplary patience. To obviate this we proceed as follows:

The first whiffing line to be put over the side is about forty yards long (and in our case it was a plaited flax line, but tastes differ in the matter of material), and its boat-shaped sinker (fitted with two swivels) is very light. I should say about two ounces. The consequence of this is that, with the motion of the yacht through the water, the said sinker is compelled to travel in the sea pretty near the surface. In fact, whenever an extra gust of wind fills in the sails and sends the yacht spinning along, the lead rises almost to the surface. Now the second line is about ten yards shorter (*i.e.* thirty yards), and its sinker weighs about five ounces, as near as I can judge. This extra weight, combined with the shortness of the line, gives the line a far greater inclination towards the bottom of the sea than the first line, with its light sinker, so that with proper management, even when hauling up the lines, there is absolutely no foul possible. And so on, for the third line. By graduating the lengths of the lines, and using proper weights, they arrive to a nicety at the object they aim at, and it is really very rare that a foul does occur. When it does, it generally happens through a strong fish performing, upon finding himself hooked, a desperate series of evolutions in all sorts of directions, when, of course, if he chances to pass over one or more of the whiffing lines, he soon gets the lot in a pretty pickle. Another thing to be guarded against, when railing lines are set in a sailing boat, is to keep a good look-out for shallows, wreckage, and seaweeds, especially when the latter are floating loose in large quantities. In the shallows, railing lines are useless, and the fisher can only come to grief by allowing them to remain in use; therefore, they should be removed the moment the bottom appears to be getting near. As regards wreckage, the plan is simply for the helmsman to give them a wide berth when the lines are out.

As regards the tell-tales, or outriggers, as they are sometimes called, they are usually simply pieces of bamboo, rigged into a notched block, fitting exactly on the gunwale. Of course the bamboo stumps project at a right angle from and over the side of the boat. The ends of these are notched, and the line fixed in that notch, or running through it. If the tell-tale is very sensitive, the moment a bite is being had the fisherman is made aware of it by the bamboo bending downwards, and coming up again two or three times running. But then you must keep your eyes on them, and if you have several actually set, the best plan is to fix on each of the outriggers, and close to the notch, a brass *grelot*; bells are apt to ring when the wind blows somewhat stiffly, therefore they give false alarms; but *grelots* require a jerk to rattle well, therefore they are to be preferred, and if the tell-tale has a good "spring," the ringing will be unmistakable. Moreover, in my opinion, the longer and more elastic the outrigger the better, as it saves a deal of casualties in the event of the line catching in weeds or other impediments, or even when a large fish is caught, when, indubitably, the "spring" of the outrigger alone saves the line from utter destruction. I therefore think that a thin and elastic piece of wood (even if projecting only two feet from the gunwale), and duly provided with a *grelot*, is far better than a stiffer piece of cane, even if five feet long, for the reasons above-mentioned. Another thing I would again beg to point out in connection with whiffing lines, and it is this: set all your fixed whiffing lines on the same side of the boat, and handle your own hand-whiffing line on the other. It will spare you a deal of bother. Should you whiff on a side where fixed whiffing lines are set, you are sure to come to a tangle sooner or later, when letting out your line or when bringing it in. It is, moreover, a moot question whether a single "set" whiffing line is not sufficient for all purposes, except, of course, when the fish are very abundant. Under ordinary circumstances, if the fisherman handles one line, and sets the other, he will find the provision quite ample for the fish to be caught. On our trip across Spithead the farthest line was the most successful of the three we had out, but the hand-line was better than the whole other three put together. At the same time, it is but fair to say that the mackerel were not quite so abundant there. Had we been below the Isle of Wight we might probably have fared better, because the largest shoals, in their journeys up Channel, keep right in it, and only a few of those shoals venture in the Solent, Southampton Water, and Spithead, except when severe weather is to be experienced in the open sea, when the fish there are rather glad than otherwise to hug the headlands for shelter. However, at sea, if it is not one sort of fish that gives you sport, there are plenty of other sorts to fall back upon, and thus we quite philosophically put up with our, at first, somewhat meagre mackerel catches.

Nevertheless, we had about two dozen when we arrived off Sea View, about eight miles' journey from Portsmouth Harbour. There we came to an anchor. It was about noon, and we instantly prepared to set a long line for flat fish over the sands. In order to save time we spliced our two long lines together, so that one set of anchors and buoys would do for both, and the three of us set about baiting it at once with lugs, mussel, mackerel, and cuttle. I cut the bait in suitable pieces, and my two friends had therefore only to fix them on the hooks. This division of labour answered admirably, and in half an hour's time our two-hundred hooked line was ready coiled, the sinkers and buoys rigged on, and we left in the dinghy to set it whilst luncheon was being prepared, and our man was laying the cloth.

About a mile from the shore we turned the dinghy's head, and I began paying out the line, whilst my two companions kept the boat going ahead slowly. I do not think, honestly, that I muddled more than half-a-dozen hooks in the two hundred, and therefore I lay the unction to my soul that the setting of long lines is not altogether an impossible accomplishment. When the final buoy was pitched overboard, we larked a bit with the boat, rowing against one another, &c., and, racing her back to the yacht, we clambered on board and went below for luncheon.

We had been at it about a quarter of an hour, more or less, when the "hand," going on deck, called out in alarm: "Wheer's the dinghy?" We rushed up and found it had vanished. Turning towards the Channel, there, half a mile from us, was the truant boat, bobbing up on the tide. "Who fastened the painter when we came aboard?" I asked of my two friends with a grin, "or rather who *pretended* to fasten it and *did not?* I am not guilty, I know, because I was second to board the yacht, therefore the first man is the guilty party." Well, they shifted the affair to one another's shoulder, and finally it was proved that the owner had done the deed. "I was *so* hungry," he pleaded in atonement, "that I wonder I even attempted to secure the boat." However, there was nothing to be done but to go in chase at once if we did not wish to lose the boat altogether, as some fisherman might have collared her, thinking she belonged to a wreck, or that some accident had happened, and there would have been the evil one to pay to get her back perhaps. Up went our jib and foresail, and we soon collared the wandering shell. This time the hand made two or three turns with the painter to make doubly sure, and we went back to our former quarters, but we had to set all sail to do it, and we were a good hour beating back, there being but little wind, and that little almost directly against us. Thus a good hour and a half was cut to waste in catching the luckless little tub. When we were back off the Nettlestone Point we resumed our lunch, but without any appetite, so that we soon agreed that the proper thing to do under the circumstances would be to lift up the long line, and forthwith sail for Chichester Harbour (a good twelve miles), wherein we could just hope to get at dark.

No time was lost in rowing off to the line, and meanwhile the sailor prepared the yacht for its journey actually by himself when we were gone, running up the jib, foresail, and mainsail, and getting up the anchor, when he came slowly our way to pick us up when we had done. We found about five dozen fish on the long line, mostly pouting, whiting, dabs, gurnards, and a multitude of crabs. Of course we did not unhook them then. We clapped the lot at the bottom of the craft, just as they came, and when we got back to the yacht we secured the dinghy astern, and I remained in it with the owner, to pick up and unhook the fish, and coil up the line for the next day's sport. This took us a good while, for it must be remembered that every hook almost required some doing. Those which had a fish were the sooner cleaned and ready. The others which had not caught were clogged with seaweeds, starfish, anemones, &c., and not a few with fish too small to keep. Well, these hooks gave us, of course, the most trouble, as we had to scrape them clean off, so that there should be no bother in the morning, when baiting them fresh. This work kept us very busy for a good hour, and we rather enjoyed the novelty of the thing; but, by Jove! how a small boat of that sort does tumble about, to be sure, over the thick heavy waves in Spithead. Our *charpente osseuse* was almost dislocated from head to foot. Banged on one side, jerked up ahead, then slack would the painter get, and at the next pull we were nearly bent in two, backwards; then on the right, then on the left, then in front, and so on, until we almost were ignorant of whether we were standing on our heads or our feet.

On the yacht, on the contrary, the motion was almost *nil*, as there was hardly any rocking to be experienced there on account of the ballast, and I strongly suspect that was why our companion had taken such good care not to undertake clearing the long line with us. It began to get dusk when we passed Fort Cumberland, but we had then only a straight run to make, and at half-past seven we were at anchor in Chichester Harbour, within a mile or two of a little village situated on the east coast of Hayling Island, and called Salterns.

Hayling Island is an irregular triangle, whose top is north and whose base is pretty fairly wholly south. The base is, I take it, about four miles wide; the apex a little more than a mile broad. It contains two decent places— North Hayling and South Hayling, with an hotel or two, a boarding establishment or two, the beginning of an esplanade, two or three large farmhouses, a few cottagers' houses, two churches; and its sands are very fine in their way. Numerous creeks lead to the island from the harbour. Some of the northern creeks are rather muddy, and I believe practically impracticable, but the southern shores are eminently fit for bathing-visitors, &c., and their children, to enjoy themselves. The neighbouring shores are noted for their oyster-beds, and, in truth, they seem eminently calculated to produce any amount of these delicious, and enormously dear and rare molluscs. The island itself is exceedingly pretty, and can be compared for peacefulness and rustic beauty to certain districts of the Isle of Wight.

For shore shooters and wildfowl shooters—*i.e.* punters, flight men, sailing shooters, &c., a stay at Hayling Island during the season would prove eminently satisfactory. When the fowl flock into the harbour, the punters have a lively time of it; after them, and in daytime, the amateur who goes about in a small boat by himself, is sure to have excellent fun with the punt-gun cripples. In the winter of 1870-1871 I bagged there, with a double 10-bore and a single 4-bore, nearly forty ducks and widgeons in five days, by merely knocking about in the creeks in daytime for single birds and cripples, and flighting at night.

In the winter 1875-1876 I also did very fairly on the tramp along the shore on the other side of the harbour, from Chichester down to West Itchenar and West Wittering. Between the two last-named villages, and about a mile from them, across the harbour, there is a little island called Pilsey, whose shores are excellent. In short, whether one keeps on either shore of the harbour or goes about Hayling Island, Morney Island, or Pilsey Island, in severe weather, the shooter is sure to have excellent fun with his wildfowl guns. Mud-splashers, however, are sometimes required there, *verb. sap.* As regards sea-fishing, there is very good fun to be had at high-tide, angling or hooking, in the very middle of the harbour. Moreover, a long line paid out at half flow, and taken up at half ebb, is sure to do well, and eels and dabs abound there. Some of the eels we caught were very good ones. We set the long line early in the morning, just by the side of the Channel, south of Pilsey Isle, and about a mile from it. Then we went hooking from the yacht and from the dinghy at the mouth of the harbour, and we had good sport. Whiting were beginning to show up; pouting came in well; gurnards were smallish, but numerous. Dabs were ravenous, and we hooked as many as we liked. At one spot, where I was by myself, I caught seventy-two in two hours. In fact, every time my line was fairly home they "rang the bell," and I had to haul up again.

I don't care much for dabs for eating, but catching them, when they are so abundant, is excellent fun, and there is only one place, to my mind, which would be about as good as Chichester Harbour for them, and that is by the side of the Kingstown West Pier, near the baths, where, one season, I used to catch near upon twelve dozen every day, and then go home. Mudworms are the proper bait for dabs, and they need not be fresh. On the contrary, I believe dabs are like those epicures who prize a pheasant if he can move on the dish when ready to be cooked.

Of "tastes and colours 'tis useless to discuss," truly. I had a little rod-fishing for eels, and also tried "bobbing" for them, but I lost many on account of not having the proper stuff wherewith to make the "ball." Bobbing for eels is extremely amusing. I remember, some years ago, having a good spin at it near Rosherville Pier in the Thames, and catching several dozens at high-tide in about an hour's time. For bobbing all the fisherman needs is a pole, a piece of twine, a few yards of worsted, and some worms, lugworms are the best. You thread the worms on the worsted, coil up the lot, fasten it in a lump with a lead to your line, fix the line to your pole, and there you are —a regular bobber, ready for active service. Dip the "worsted lot" until you touch bottom, then raise it slightly, and at once, if eels are about, they will bite at the bait.

Now comes the fun of the thing. There is no hook whatsoever, be it borne in mind, in the whole concern; but the eels are so pertinacious, and they hold so tightly, and their teeth are so sharp, that the worsted fairly hooks their teeth, and if you proceed smartly in hauling them up you will find that they will be unable to release themselves until, having them safely in your boat or on land, you jerk them loose from your tackle. So you see, reader, the trick, like most good tricks, is wonderfully simple, and as to its success, why it is simply admirable. Many men have had statues erected to their memory who did not deserve them half so well as the inventor of "bobbing for eels."

At Chichester Harbour you can bob for eels by the hour, and when your skill has reached its *apogee* it is immensely entertaining. You can always tell, with a little experience, how many eels are on, and several times I have had six on my bait at one and the same time. Of course they varied greatly in size, some being like pencils and others like congers. All the small ones were carefully put aside to be returned to the sea when the play was over, as otherwise they will come again and again to the tackle fifty times over, as though they rather enjoyed the process of being hoisted through air and water, and inspecting the internal economy of a fishing-boat. Thus varying the fun in many different ways, we spent a most pleasant day near Hayling Island. The long line was well "hung" with sundry fine fish, and our respective whiffing, hooking, angling, and bobbing were, on their individual merits, very entertaining.

Altogether, in our two days, we used five shillings' worth of bait, or at the rate of one shilling and eightpence each! Surely this cannot be called costly sport!

BARN ROCKS, BOGNOR ROCKS, AND THE PARK.

We had all sorts of incidents during our cruise, although on the afternoon of the first day we had to fly for shelter behind Selsea Bill.

To begin at the beginning, the yacht, with my two companions on board, had sailed from Chichester Harbour during the night and reached Bognor in the morning. The yacht of course remained away at sea, about a mile from the pier, and the sailor with one of my friends came in the dinghy to fetch me.

I had arrived by train and was watching for them impatiently, for, the morning was delicious, and I had had more than half a mind to accept the offers of sundry fishermen to go with them fishing in their boats.

At last I spied the yacht coming from the Park, and an hour afterwards I was on board, and we then headed back for the Barn Rocks where we intended beginning sport.

My friends had secured a great lot of lugs. I am afraid to say how many they had; but a large pail was full of them, well packed in mud, seaweed, and salt water, the right way to preserve them in fine condition, for at least two or three days. Whilst we were sailing to the rocks I went below to manufacture a special line, and my companions, much interested, came to see what I was about.

"Young congers," said I, " are now showing up. They are not so big as to need a regular conger line. Yet it must be strong enough to resist their teeth, so I intend making a special line, and fishing with a small hook."

Saying this, I rigged up a line with copper wire from the hook to the line proper, but instead of having half-a-dozen wires to constitute the conger-proof snood, I only twisted three, and placed a large-eyed hook at the bottom. They proceeded in the same manner, and when we reached our anchorage about a mile from the shore, we were ready for the fray. The tide setting in very strong, we found that our weights were far from being sufficiently heavy, so that delayed us still more. Not to be in the way of my companions I hauled up the dinghy, and settled myself therein comfortably. My two friends had caught respectively a pouting and a conger before I began in earnest. I found a great deal of water where we stood, over a deep hole probably, and this made me fear for my light tackle, for old and powerful congers generally inhabit these strong fastnesses, and of course if a monster had laid hold of my 3-wire snood, there would not have been much hope of its holding it long in safety.

Said the owner presently: "I have got a lot of bites!"

"Ah!" returned another with a wink at me, "'They all do it,' you know."

"Ay, ay!" exclaimed I, jerking up a conger on the floor of my little craft, "'and some rue it,' too!"

My conger was very perverse. Not content with a

hook, a lug, and four inches of copper snooding, he tried to swallow one of the sculls. At least I suppose he wanted to do so, as he deliberately seized it when I placed my foot on his neck, and it was a job to rid him of my property. When liberated I dashed him to the floor with a terrific whack, but he seemed all the more lively for it, went up towards the stern, and began rummaging amongst the boards there. I left him to that entertaining pursuit.

Shortly after I was lighting a pipe when one of my chums, seated on the combing of the yacht, called out joyfully that he had something on. I felt my line too, and found it heavy.

"So have I," cried I, and I began hauling in and he ditto.

"By Jove! the weight increases, but there are no perceptible wriggles. What the deuce can it be? Oh! a crab, no doubt."

But about halfway up I come to a dead stand, and my comrade also. He pulls, I pull, and we then find that our lines are mixed. He was a good twenty feet distance from me, but such was the force of the stream that his lead had been seized in a whirlpool which landed it in my hole right by the side of mine. Then, of course, what with the eddies, whirlpools, and the stream of tide, the two lines had got into some slight confusion.

"Haul them both in," cried he, "in your dinghy; you will have a better chance of clearing them without breaking anything than I. If I tried I might break a hook when hoisting the lot over the gun'ale."

"All right," I said, and he slackening his line, I was enabled to bring up the lot; but just when I was going to hoist them aboard, snap went something, and his line ran down again. It was all right, but my friend's hook was caught in my lead, and the snood had broken away from the line. In a minute or two he had repaired the damage, and was soon again at it, but taught by experience, he put on a heavier lead. I must certainly have drained my hole of congers, for at last not another bite could I get after I had caught about half-a-dozen ; but when in despair I threw a handful of lugs down, so as to attract fish in my neighbourhood, I caught them to any extent, but no more congers.

My argument on the point is this : Originally the holes under the rocks where I was fishing were tenanted by say half-a-dozen congers, and no other fish. All these I caught, but when I "ground-baited," a lot of higher-swimming fish came to the spot, and filled up the place in the room of those fishes that had been taken. Has any other sea-fisherman noticed such a change?

My first catch, after baiting, was a turbot, a superb fish. When I glanced over the side of the dinghy to see what I had on that was so heavy, my heart almost jumped in my mouth. "I shall never get him out," I thought, but by judiciously hauling in, and letting go, I brought the fish within a foot of the surface. I could do no more then, for when I tried to lift him up, I found that the moment he reached the air, my line was totally unable to cope against such an increase of "dead drag," and so, perforce, I had to manœuvre scientifically. Holding the line pretty taut in my left hand, I crawled forward until I reached the painter and keeping my eye on the turbot, I hauled up on the painter gently, meanwhile telling my friends to hand me the gaff. The sailor had been watching me all the time, and suddenly tumbling into the dinghy with one of the wildfowl nets, he slipped it under the fish, and even then he had his work cut out to secure him. A turbot is not caught every day. This one overlapped the net on all sides, and everybody on board smacked his lips at the sight of him. After wiping my forehead, for this tussle with the turbot had warmed me, I bethought myself that my hole ought to have been well baited, and accordingly threw my line in again.

Then I went to the stern to see if anything was on the line there. There was a hake. A regular beast though, for after a good deal of trouble it broke our "communicator" and was gone! Replacing a snood and hook, and casting the line over took me some little time. When I had finished, my other line appeared uncommonly taut. I tumbled to it, and found another fish there, a pouting.

The other line now runs out! I always leave a lot of line on the seat, and there can be no mistake when the line is run out by a fish, for it goes then by yards at a jump, whereas when the boat sheers it only takes a little of the line out, and that little not very fast. The stern line had a pouting. Then it caught another hake. The other line had a small brill, then a pouting, then another, then a conger.

My companions were also getting on well, and we were thoroughly enjoying ourselves, when "Crack! crack! crack! boom! boom! boom!" the Russians and the Turks are at it, by Jove! and we look up. It was simply a storm. And such a lively storm, too! The lightning flashed vividly, and things began to look so bad, that I went aboard, and we all sat down below, before our dinner, whilst outside the Turks and the Russians were at it hammer and tongs.

Presently in came the man, clad in "yellow" from head

to toes, and looking uncommonly like the hippopotamus at the Zoo when it leaves its bath.

"There'll be a wind presently," said he, looking to windward.

"Which way does the wind come from?" I asked, with my mouth full, for I was not much disturbed, knowing the boat to be a right trustworthy little yacht.

"From N.W.," said the "hand."

"Well, then, let us run behind Selsea Bill for shelter," resumed I; "we will ride it out there. It won't last long. An April shower, and a blow now and then, that is all. We shall be all right enough."

"Right you are," said the owner cheerily. "Turn out, all hands, to make sail," shouted he then, as though we had been on board a man-of-war.

"Ay, ay, yer honour," said we, laughing, and on deck we tumbled like a lot of ants going on a foraging expedition. In a trice all sail was set, the anchor was up, and we were labouring towards the Bill. How the boat plunged, and how drenched she was and we were! The waves rode fiercely towards her, but she gaily forged through them, slapping heavily on the low ones, and grinding the top ones into foam.

"Whish!" went the wind into the rigging; "whish!" went the sea against the counters; and "hough! hough!" roared the yacht, flailing the turmoiling waters into soapsuds, and thus we went on, the three of us in the cockpit admiring the scene, and holding tight when the lee-scuppers went under, which they did half-a-dozen times every minute.

What an hour we had of it! At last we reached shelter, ran in as far as the wind would take us, and then we rode it out very nicely. We turned in as soon as the sea ran tolerably smooth, as we did not wish to be shot out of our berths. Early in the morning I woke up, and found the yacht riding very steadily. I listened, there were a few "tell-tales" murmuring along the counters, but there was no longer any whistling in our rigging, and I went on deck to look around. The sun was just appearing, somewhere Beachy Head way—the next headland to us—and I thought that we might as well start. The man was forward, mopping away, and doing the yacht's morning toilet as usual. "Shall I run up the jib and pick up anchor, sir," said he, "we need not wake the master or his friend?" In the midst of our preparations, however, both of them turned up too, and we sailed to Bognor Rocks, about five miles, in an hour's time, dropped anchor two miles from the pier, and then went below to breakfast. This over, we bent all our energies to hooking. From nine A.M. till four P.M. we could not find time to have a meal. I rushed into the cabin at about twelve almost famished. Two biscuits and a pint of sherry set me right. The fish came in very fast, we had no disaster worth mentioning, and when evening drew near a more tired lot than we were could hardly have been found. We slept like tops. The man kept watch, and looked after our riding light throughout the night, and but for this attention I believe we should have been run down by a screw collier, which passed quite close to us, blowing its whistle, at about three A.M., when the rain fell so fast as to almost obscure our whereabouts. Next day we went farther away into the Channel. None of us tried railing, as it was a moot question whether any mackerel were about, and as we knew that any amount of bottom-fishing could be had, we did not trouble our heads about whiffing lines. I should not like to specify, within two score, how many fish we caught during the three days. All I know is, that for my share I had over one hundred and fifty good-sized ones, and I have rarely spent half a week in more pleasurable quarters. Hake, brill, turbot, gurnard, pouting, crabs, whiting, thornbacks, were in profusion. Let my readers try the spot, and they will do well to provide plenty of hampers if they wish to take their catches home.

BOULOGNE-SUR-MER.

I WENT down to Dover to meet my companions for a quiet cruise over the rocky bottoms and a short spin in the Channel for mackerel; but scarcely were we under weigh, at half-past six A.M., than half a gale got up, and we had to think about going back. This, however, was sooner thought of than performed, for the wind was N.E., and blowing great guns; so, Dover being out of the question, we thought of running into Folkestone. When about halfway there, the sea moderated, and our owner declared that we could have a fine spin across the Channel if we liked. This wild notion found favour. I had not been over to the French coast for some time, and our companion being also willing and delighted, we turned her head south-east, and away we went. The journey across was devoid of incident. We saw many vessels making the most of the wind to drop down Channel; there were also plenty of fishing-smacks about, and we saw steamers innumerable forging their way up and down the Channel. At about two P.M. we passed Cape Grisnez on our port side, and its majestic lighthouse, rising like a tower of strength on the cliffs, suggested to us the query as to with what success the submarine railway was meeting.

At half-past five we entered Boulogne harbour. The old town was just the same; the fishwives still wear their quaint caps and long gold earrings, the soldiery still rejoice in their wide red breeches, the gendarmes still look upon foreigners with a suspicious eye, the Customs officers still imagine that every British boat is bent on smuggling something or other into the French territory, the crowds still gather at the arrival of the steamers, women still wheel goods on their barrows to the station, and there is still a very large colony of English families residing in the town and its suburbs.

When we had dropped our anchor, a French customs officer came aboard for the usual queries, and looked very dubious when we told him we only came for fishing. However, he had to be content with that explanation, as it was the true one; but when he went away he shrugged his shoulders, and said to his men, "*Ces Anglais sont fous!*" It is a remarkable thing that everywhere the enthusiastic pursuit of sport on the part of Englishmen is looked upon by foreigners as a sure sign of incipient lunacy, and when we went ashore the officials seemed to regard us as regular "Hanwellites."

We had no difficulty in getting abundance of bait, and it was remarkably cheap too. There were several score of smacks in harbour with a rare lot of fish, and when we inquired at one of these for fresh mackerel and other etceteras for bait, the skipper said, "What for? fishing?" And on our answering in the affirmative, he seemed to be quite proud, and insisted that we should have as much bait as we wanted, gratis! This we would not agree to, of course, and so we bestowed on his lad what we would have given for the commodities he brought us.

So many tourists find their way annually to Boulogne that it may be interesting to them to know what sort of sport in the sea-fishing line is to be had there. British visitors to Calais, Boulogne, Dieppe, Trouville, St. Malo, Brest, and other French watering-places, during the season, are to be reckoned by thousands; and often have I had inquiries as to what sort of sport was to be had there in the hook as well as in the gun line. Therefore my information is sure to prove very acceptable, and were it possible, I would readily visit the principal of these places, and give my experience thereof. If I can manage to take a run over during the summer months I will certainly do so. Meanwhile, let me treat of Boulogne. As to sport, the shootings are getting more and more into the hands of the natives, who begin to be alarmed at the influx of English shooters, and wish to make them pay for the sport they get, just as the Norwegians are going to attempt to do. Still, from what I gleaned, there is some field of free action yet left open; but it requires search and a little cash, perhaps. The fishing in the river Liane, at Pont de Briggues (two or three miles from Boulogne), is still come-at-able; but "first come, first served," there. As for the sea-fishing, it is admirable, and there are lots of boats, and armies of boatmen ready to take the enthusiastic hooker over the deep.

I met a party of three Englishmen who had just come ashore, after a trip of a week in the Channel in one of the

French fishing-boats. They described their treatment as excellent. The men attended well to their wants, and were delighted to have them on board. They trawled, and used also drift nets, and thoroughly enjoyed themselves. The after-cabin had been cleared especially for their use, and for the whole trip they were charged about two sovereigns. They also told me that they frequently hired a cobble, with a man, and went shrimping in the season, and the rest of the time they go hooking along the coast.

From them I picked up some information as to the best spots where fish loved to congregate; and I took a hint as to the desirability of not attempting to go fishing by ourselves. "The coast," they said, "is dangerous to a stranger, on account of the many belts of rock which abound there. As for the Boulogne boatmen, they know every nook and corner from their infancy, and they take good care to have no accident, for the very excellent reason that, as each man owns the boat he sails in, and the said boat constitutes all his worldly possessions and his only means of living, he is mighty careful not to so much as grate her keel anywhere, and a good thing too." I quite agreed with them that, under the circumstances, sailing a ballasted yacht would be a sheer act of folly, and we went to arrange with a man for the morrow. The cobble we secured was a stout craft, with full beam, and our weather-beaten tar was voluble in his promises to show us sport.

In the evening we strolled on the jetty, and the night being fine, we found a goodly company assembled there, although the season was yet so early. Two or three lads were hooking from the end of the jetty, but they caught only small fish, the tide being anything but sufficiently high to bring near the larger denizens of the deep.

Early in the morning we were off. The sky was cloudy, and the wind being directly against us when we left the harbour, we hired another fellow to do the rowing with our man. They took us in a northern direction along the coast. They rowed about a mile until we reached the neighbourhood of an old stone fort, built in the sea by Napoleon I. when he meant to invade England. The bottom round about there is of the very rockiest description.

"Lots of fish here," said our men, as they dropped overboard a stone for our moorings, and we got ready. We had for bait herrings, mackerel, and squid. I thought mackerel would be best of all, and stuck to it, but perceived no remarkable difference between my catches and those of my two comrades. There were lots of congers about, and the pouting towards the latter end of our stay were also very numerous. The men fished as much as we did. Knowing that all that was caught was to be theirs, they were wonderfully sharp, and exhibited an extraordinary aptitude for hooking, the second man we had engaged catching something or other every time he let his line down. He seemed to have pitted himself against us, and though he never addressed us, his remarks to his elderly companion fully convinced us of that fact, and the gist of his remarks was to the purport that, for hooking, there was no nation in the world that could beat the French.

"The English," said he, *sotto voce*, to his chum, "let the

fish hook itself. What a mistake! You should hook the fish!" Certainly he joined practice to theory, for he did hook them with a vengeance. There he was, standing in the bows, with his breeches right over his guernsey, and his sou'-wester in his back, chewing away his 'baccy, and holding his line high up in the air, then up his hand went. "Here is another," and sure enough, he had another, and sometimes two, and not uncommonly three. "I could be at this sort of game day and night," said he, and I believe that readily. This fellow comes from Guernsey, where everybody, more or less, from five years old upwards, is an artist at hooking. We shifted our position twice, and every time the fish answered to the roll-call.

When we were tired of the spot the men took us opposite the mouth of a small stream which runs through a village called Wimille. The bottom there was a mixture of pebbles, sand, mud, and rocks, and through the river emptying itself there, a good many fish, flat and otherwise, congregated about to get their share of the spoils brought down by the soft water into the sea. By-the-way, there were a great number of black-ducks and divers about there, but of widgeon and ducks not one did I see. We began hooking at that spot as soon as the boat had settled to her moorings, and my first fish was a fine dab. The next catch was a pouting, caught by my friend, whilst the sailors had each a dab. We drifted out, finding our fish small, and we again evidently got into rocky ground, for the pouting and conger became thick and quick, and hake, brill, and turbot were in turn secured. We were three hours there.

"Could we not land anywhere about here?" I inquired

of our man, after a consultation with my friends. "Oh yes!" they said, "the sea is smooth, we could row the boat right in-shore on the sands, and haul her up." "All right, then," said Thompson, "do so; my friend says there is a *café* or two close by in the village. Is that right?" "Yes, sir, quite right; there are two or three," replied the old tar. "One is the Snipe Shooter's Inn, and the other one the Shooter's Inn. We landed and wended our way to the nearest inn, which happened to be the Sportsman's. Over a wooden bridge we went, and found the inn looking very clean, neat, and appetising. They had no fresh meat, however, but an *omelette sautée*, scientifically cooked, and a bottle of claret did duty for it, and after a good cigar, we felt quite ready to go to sea again, and we followed back our two tars.

It was about two P.M. then, and I thought that we should do well to extend our excursion a little farther, and then make tracks back for the harbour, as I wanted to return by the mail steamer to Folkestone, and my two friends would sail back at their leisure on the following day. We therefore made our next sitting as complete an affair as we could, anchoring in a deep part about a mile from shore, and as this was to be our last chance we baited copiously, and had as good a bit of sport as the men's promises had led us to believe. The place, however, was positively infested with dog-fish, both small and large, and more than once one of them made a rush at one of our fish, and escaped being caught. We nevertheless managed to bring two good-sized and a small one to book, and a good riddance it was. The Frenchmen, however, did not wish the fish to be thrown away, and they averred that there is a market for these dainties (?) in Boulogne. I wonder with what sauce they may be prepared in order to make them palatable, for they look very oily at best.

One of the men caught two fine brill, a good-sized hake, and lost another, which was a veritable monster. The conger, however, gave us the best sport, and it did not take much to induce them to bite, but we kept on moving a few yards away, now and then, after a few catches, the men agreeing with me that it is better to do so for rock-fish. It seems, however, that as a rule French fishermen are content with trawling and netting, at least near Boulogne, for we did not see anyone about, hooking, but there were plenty of trawlers and drift-netters farther up the Channel. Yet I fancy that half-a-dozen open boats, hooking where we were, would have done exceedingly well, judging from the results of our excursion.

There are lots of cuttle-fish, which the French call *pieuvres*, and we caught five or six. I had two decent-sized ones myself. Our men believed in the great Victor Hugo's notion about monstrous *pieuvres*, and said that they had heard vaguely about one dragging a man to the bottom of the sea. It cannot be denied that, if squid can reach such enormous sizes as has been asserted, a man would fare very badly indeed when once within their arms. The other fish were middling-sized. Not a single mackerel did we see.

Sometimes, when the tide is at its highest, very good fun is to be had from the jetties. On both sides of the harbour at Boulogne, of course, one has to fish on their lee for good sport. Strange to say, the French inhabitants of the town, or its French visitors, rarely take to sea-hooking for sport. When they wish to have a little fishing they engage a fishing-smack or a boat, and tell the men to carry on their calling in their presence, finding it entertaining to watch their proceedings, and preferring to stand by and look on, rather than wet their hands with hooking, and get fish-scales on their boots. This is carried to such an extent that the men stated it as a fact that nine out of ten parties which, during the season hire them for hooking trips, are exclusively composed of Englishmen. I quite believe that. But if the French dislike wetting their hands and soiling their fine clothes, why do they not hook with rods? I believe that wrinkle is, as yet, a mystery to them; but if they take as heartily to sea-fishing as they have done to horse-racing, they won't be slow to devise means, and then possibly, as in the other sport, they may prove very successful rivals. I do not despair of seeing such a thing come to pass.

At Ostend dip-nets are regularly rigged on the jetty for the season, and it is actually the height of fashion for the visitors to have a turn at them every day. Once (three years ago) I was with a friend handling such an instrument on the west jetty, and our right-hand neighbour was no less a personage than the daughter of the late King Victor Emmanuel; on our left was a grand duke, and farther on were other notabilities of high rank.

Now, why do not the French and English boatmen at watering-places follow the example given them by the Belgians, and rig out affairs of the same kind? If it may induce them to do so, I can state as a matter of £ s. d. that these Belgian letters of nets pocket pounds daily with nets which hardly cost them more than one or two sovereigns to rig out complete. I told our men all this, and it made them open their eyes.

I can confidently recommend visitors to Boulogne to try sea-fishing there. I shall not lose sight of my proposal to visit sundry other places on the Continental coasts, and at the first favourable opportunity I will report on their capabilities.

THE END.

www.ingramcontent.com/pod-product-compliance
Lightning Source LLC
Chambersburg PA
CBHW031945230426
43672CB00010B/2056